ALMOST EVERYTHING ABOUT GUITAR CHORDS

A fun, systematic, constructive, informative
approach to the study of chords.

Ralph Louis Scicchitano

ALMOST EVERYTHING ABOUT GUITAR CHORDS
A FUN, SYSTEMATIC, CONSTRUCTIVE, INFORMATIVE
APPROACH TO THE STUDY OF CHORDS.

iUniverse books may be ordered through booksellers or by contacting:

iUniverse
1663 Liberty Drive
Bloomington, IN 47403
www.iuniverse.com
1-800-Authors (1-800-288-4677)

*Because of the dynamic nature of the Internet, any web addresses or
links contained in this book may have changed since publication and may
no longer be valid. The views expressed in this work are solely those
of the author and do not necessarily reflect the views of the publisher,
and the publisher hereby disclaims any responsibility for them.*

*Any people depicted in stock imagery provided by Getty Images are models,
and such images are being used for illustrative purposes only.
Certain stock imagery © Getty Images.*

ISBN: 978-1-5320-9930-4 (sc)
ISBN: 978-1-5320-9931-1 (e)

Library of Congress Control Number: 2020906896

Print information available on the last page.

iUniverse rev. date: 09/23/2020

PREFACE

Guitarists, perhaps more than any other instrumentalist, tend to think of chords as a separate entity of music. Even advanced players are often called upon to perform in an accompaniment role using mostly movable chord forms (chord forms without open strings). Knowledge of these is most important to the improvisor and soloist as well.

Until now, a good method for chord study has not been available. Previous studies had little or no information on the relationship chords have within the framework of a key or chord progression. Often, time is wasted on unorganized studies that provide little or no information on chord construction. This method does not try to cover every chord, or the many different ways of playing chords with the same name. Almost Everything About Guitar Chords is primarily concerned with quick mastering of two movable chord forms for each chord name: one with the root on the ⑥ string and one with the root on the ⑤ string. It will systematically direct you to the strongest, most useful, and often easiest chord forms. It will teach you construction and evolution along with memorization. Exercises for each group contain harmonic analyses, which show you how the chords relate. This is extremely valuable knowledge that other methods seldom cover.

One of the biggest psychological problems students have when learning a musical instrument is in underestimating the amount of effort involved in practicing. That is why the lessons in this method should be supplemented with tunes, as a motivational force. However, to avoid unrealistic expectations, just remember that a true love and joy for good things like music comes with practice, time and patience. Do not expect instant gratification.

To my wife Sue, Don Bouchard and Matt Derby

whose support made this work possible.

TABLE OF CONTENTS

HOW TO READ THIS METHOD

Roman numerals are used to identify how chords function within a key. Chords are built from each scale degree. Some are used more often than others. This method will cover some of the more common progressions. Using the key of [C] for example, here are the diatonic chords:

You can see that many of these chords have some of the same notes: C and Am, Dm and F, Em and G, Em and C, G and B dim (diminished). Sometimes these can be substituted for creative purposes.

The numbers inside the diagrams represent scale degrees that make up the chords. The numbers underneath the diagrams are the fingers. The fingers on the left hand are numbered 1 for the pointer, 2 for the middle finger, 3 for the ring finger, and 4 for the pinky. Numbers in parenthesis are optional bass notes. "X" denotes deadened strings. The fret position is determined by the finger farthest to the left.

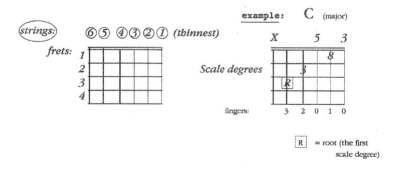

CHAPTER ONE

> *OPEN POSITION CHORDS, CHORD CONSTRUCTION, CHORD FUNCTION and COMMON CHORD TENDENCIES.*

LESSON ONE: *The I and V chords (tonic and dominant)*

A good beginning exercise involves the I and V chords in the key of [C]. The I-V, in various keys, is the most basic chord format or progression. Dozens of songs use it; "He's Got The Whole World In His Hands", "Down In The Valley", and "Tom Dooley" to name a few. The I chord is a MAJOR TRIAD made up of the 1 (R and 8), 3 and 5 scale degrees. The V chord is built from the V degree of the scale; R, 3, 5, and usually the ♭7.

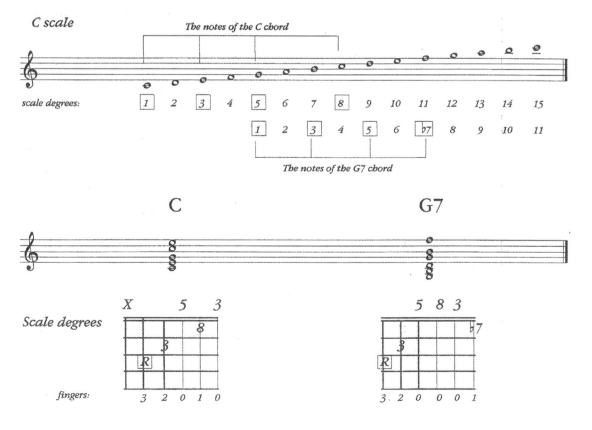

In EXERCISE ONE, hit the bass note string on the first beat and then strum the remainder of the strings on the second and third beats (the ④ ③ ② ① strings). This is a waltz or three beat strum. Practice the exercise <u>slowly</u> and steadily. Strive to change the chords without hesitation. To keep up momentum when changing chords try this order of movement:

(1) Move the top fingers

(2) Hit the bass

(3) Move the first finger

(4) Strum the remaining strings

<u>EXERCISE ONE:</u>

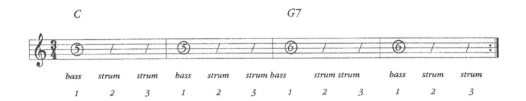

LESSON TWO: The I - IV - V chord progression. (tonic - sub dominant - dominant)

The most common chord progression in music is the I - IV - V. For this, we will work in the key of [G]. This is a good time to point out the tendency for the V chord to resolve or progress to the I chord. Exceptions do occur however, especially in blues.

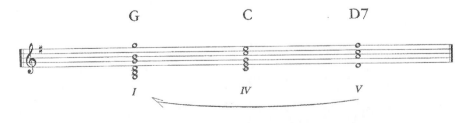

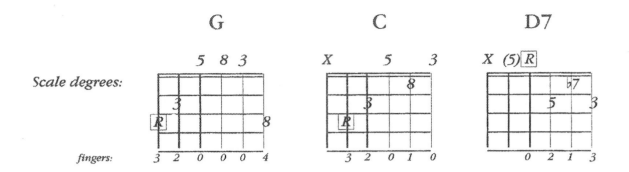

Here is a list of songs using only the I – IV – V chords:

"SILENT NIGHT"

"SHE'LL BE COMING AROUND THE MOUNTAIN"

"OH SUSANA"

"GOOD NIGHT LADIES"

"HARK! THE HERALD ANGELS SING"

"OLD MACDONALD HAD A FARM"

In EXERCISE TWO, Practice the key of [G] chord progression. Strum each of the chords once. Strive to keep steady time and to eventually be able to change chords without hesitation. Practice all exercises until they are mastered.

Exercise Two:

play: G   C   G   D7   G   C   D7   G

        I   *IV*   *I*   *V*   *I*   *IV*   *V*   *I*

OPTIONAL EAR TRAINING EXERCISE:

Tune your voice to a G chord and try some of the songs from the list. Sing the melody and strum a G chord until you hear the chord change. It will change to either a C or D7. If you make the wrong choice, it will not go with the melody that you are singing. Use a down stroke for each beat. With experience, you will become more proficient at this. In time you will be able to "listen ahead" and anticipate the chord changes with better accuracy.

Example:

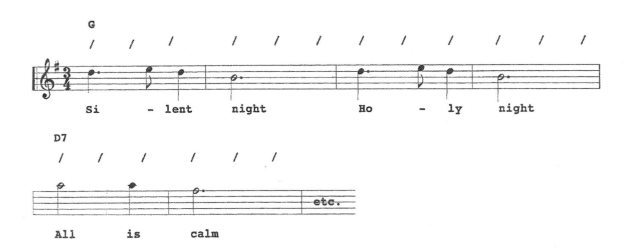

LESSON THREE: *The vim chord*

This chord is built from the 6ᵗʰ degree of the scale. It is important to know that <u>all</u> minor chords have a ♭3 scale degree. To untrained ears the vim chord will often sound very similiar to the I chord. Bass movement can make a big difference.

<u>Example</u>: Key of [G]

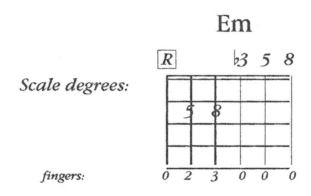

Em

Scale degrees:

fingers:

<u>*Exercise Three:*</u>   *Hold your fingers down as much as possible.*

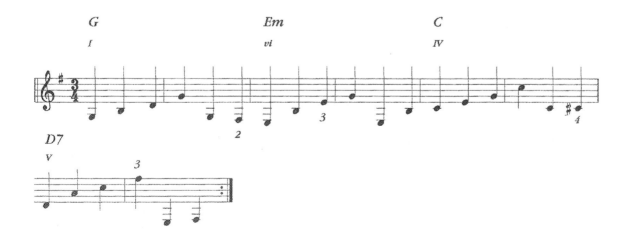

LESSON FOUR: *Secondary dominant 7th chords*

In addition to the I chord (tonic), any other diatonic chord can have its own "personal" V chord (dominant). These are chords a little harder to hear than the I - IV - V sequence. They are commonly used however, and will ring an "aural bell", as you acquire some experience with them. Some of the more common secondary dominants are; The V/IV, Example: In the key of [G] the chord progression; G - G7 - C - D7 - G, (G7) has the accidental (f♮) and will usually resolve to the IV chord (C) . Another commonly used secondary dominant is the V/V. Example: In the chord progression; G - A7 - D7 - G, (A7) has the accidental (c#) and will usually resolve to D7.

Example: Key of [G].

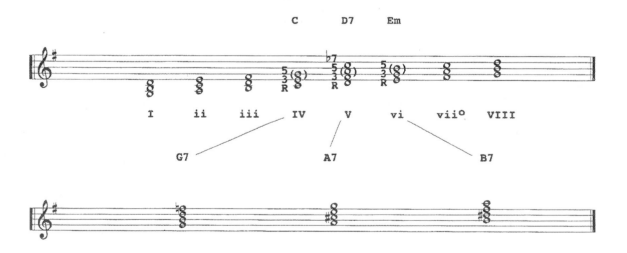

This is the chord that is built from the 5th degree of the IV chord.

V/IV

This is the chord that is built from the 5th degree of the V chord.

V/V

This is the chord that is built from the 5th degree of the vi chord.

V/vi

Here is a list of some well known songs that have secondary dominant 7th chords.

"AURA LEE"	V/V V/vi
"BICYCLE BUILT FOR TWO"	V/V
"BILL BAILEY"	V/IV
"DIXIE"	V/V
"IT CAME UPON A MIDNIGHT CLEAR"	V/V V/vi
"JINGLE BELLS"	V/V
"OH COME ALL YE FAITHFUL"	V/V
"O HOLY NIGHT"	V/iii

In EXERCISE FIVE, we will use a four beat (common time) strum. Hit the primary bass note (root) on the first beat, and then strum the remainder of the chord on the 2nd, 3rd, and 4th beat.

Exercise Five:

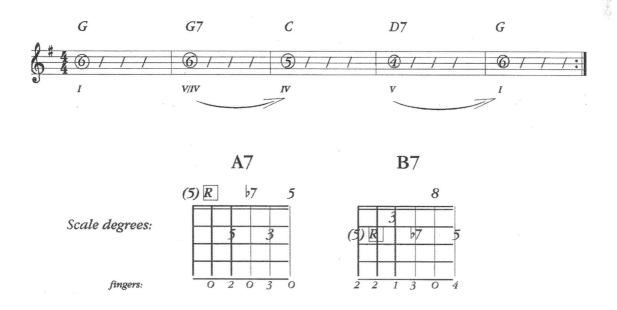

Exercise Six: _Strum once for each chord._

play: G   B7   Em   C   A7   D7   G

I   V/vi   vi   IV   V/V   V   I

LESSON FIVE: _Some of the more common chords in the key of [Am]._

Minor keys are usually based on the HARMONIC MINOR scale. This scale has the raised 7th degree, which accounts for the (g#) in the E7 chord.

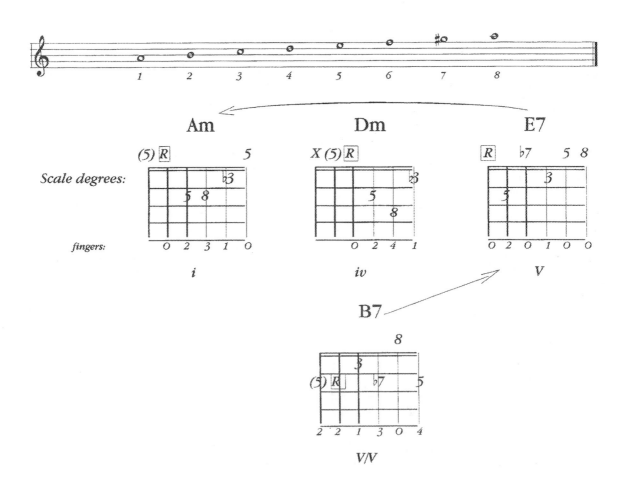

Scale degrees:

fingers:

Am — i

Dm — iv

E7 — V

B7 — V/V

- 8 -

Exercise Seven: *Strum once each.*

Am   E7   Am   Dm   Am   Dm   E7   Am   B7   E7   Am

i   V   i   iv   i   iv   V   i   V/V   V   i

LESSON SIX: *Some of the more common chords in the key of [D].*

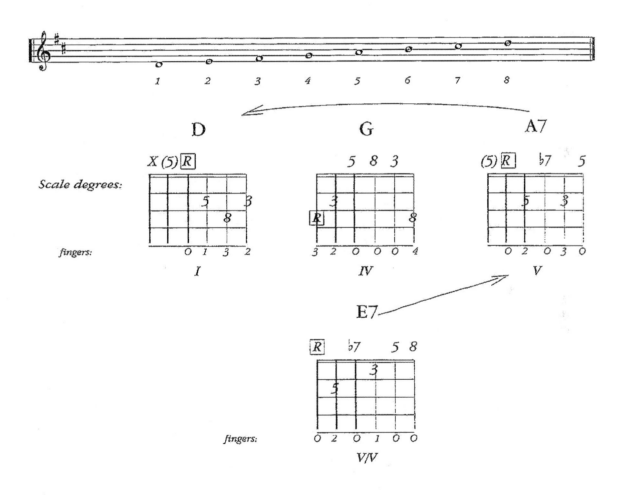

- 9 -

Exercise Eight: *Strum once each.*

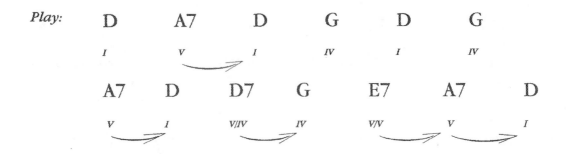

Play: D   A7   D   G   D   G

       I   *V*   *I*   *IV*   *I*   *IV*

      A7   D   D7   G   E7   A7   D

       V   *I*   *V/IV*   *IV*   *V/V*   *V*   *I*

LESSON SEVEN: *Some of the more common chords in the key of [A].*

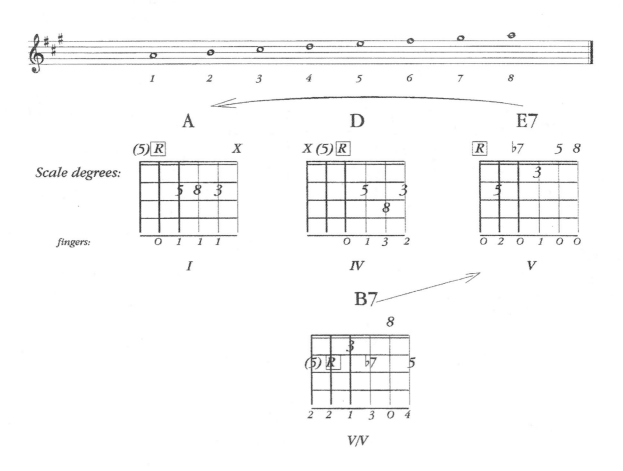

Scale degrees:

     A   D   E7

fingers:

     I   *IV*   *V*

                 B7

               V/V

Exercise Nine: *Strum once each.*

Play:

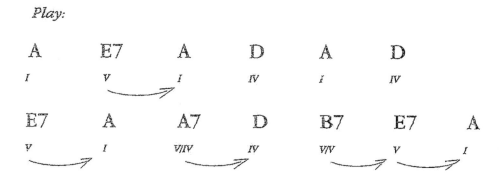

LESSON EIGHT: *Optional music theory lesson.*

This lesson may be better suited to a music theory class than applied directly to the guitar fingerboard. However, to have greater knowledge of chord construction, let's take another look at the harmonized major scale:

Example: Key of [G]

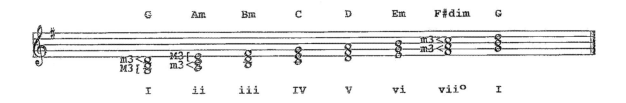

These chords are called triads because they are constructed of only three notes: the root (1), 3 and 5 degrees. The 1 and 8 are usually considered to be the same.

The notes are stacked in 3rds above the chord root. Notice that when the root of the chord is on a staff line, the 3rd and 5th will be placed on the lines above. When the chord root is on a space, the 3rd and 5th are on the spaces above. The exact 3rd intervals are marked. A major 3rd is (2) steps (four frets up), a minor third is 1 1/2 steps up.

These chords are in root position; that is, with the 1st scale degree in the bass. However, you can have inversions, with other chord notes in the bass.

Here is the harmonized scale in first inversion (3rd degree in the bass):

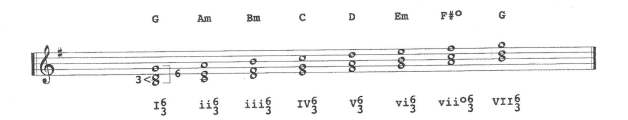

The designation $\binom{6}{3}$, for the 1st inversion, is from traditional music theory. This signifies the intervals up from the bottom note. The numbers $\binom{6}{4}$ are for the 2nd inversion, that inversion has the 5th degree in the bass.

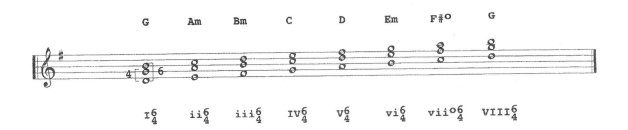

With guitar chord symbols, we usually don't refer to $\binom{6}{3}$ or $\binom{6}{4}$ for chord inversions. We usually write the chord symbol and then the precise bass note if we want a note other than the root in the bass.

Example:

C/E   is a (C) chord with the 3rd (E) in the bass.
G/D   is a (G) chord with the 5th (D) in the bass.

Depending on the style of music, it is often more common to play chords with the addition of a 7th degree (a 3rd above the 5th).

Here is the harmonized scale in 7th chords:

Example: Key of [G].

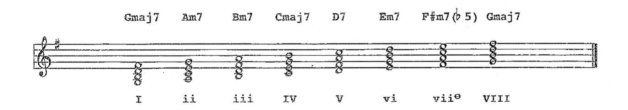

It is advisable to write out and memorize the harmonized scale with 7th chords in all keys.

LESSON NINE: _The remaining open position chords, review and_ _advancement exam._

On the following pages you will find a review of the open position chords covered in this chapter, along with a few new ones. Almost any chord not found in this lesson would be better played with movable forms. The choice between open position and movable forms however, usually depends on the strategic situation and (or) the sound that you are looking for. Movable chord forms are when one finger formation is used to produce many of the same type of chord by moving up or down the fingerboard.

Again, the numbers in the diagrams are the scale degrees. Any MAJOR chord (for example: G, C, A etc.) is made up of only the 1 (root), 3, and 5 scale degrees. MINOR chords (for example: Gm, Cm, Am etc.) is made up of only the 1 (root), ♭ 3, and 5 degrees. MAJOR 7th chords (for example: G maj.7, Cmaj.7, Amaj.7 etc.) is made up of the root, 3, 5, and 7th. DOMINANT 7th chords (for example: G7, C7, A7 etc.) is made up of the root, 3, 5 and ♭ 7. MINOR 7th chords (for example: Gm7, Cm7, Am7 etc.) is made up of the root, ♭3, 5, and ♭ 7. SUSPENDED 4 chords (for example; Gsus4, Csus4, Asus4 etc.) is made up of the root, 4, and 5th.

Memorize the scale degree constuction of each type of chord.

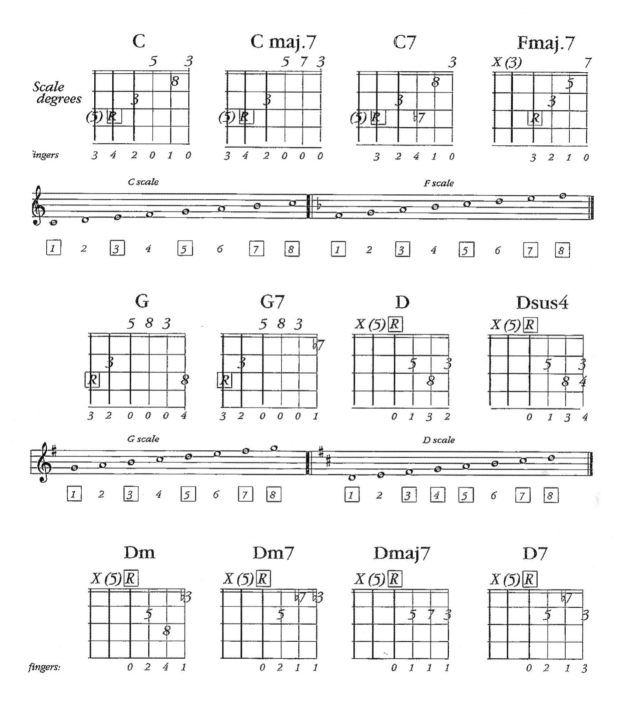

* Before Proceeding to the next group of chords, master quiz 1 on page 18.

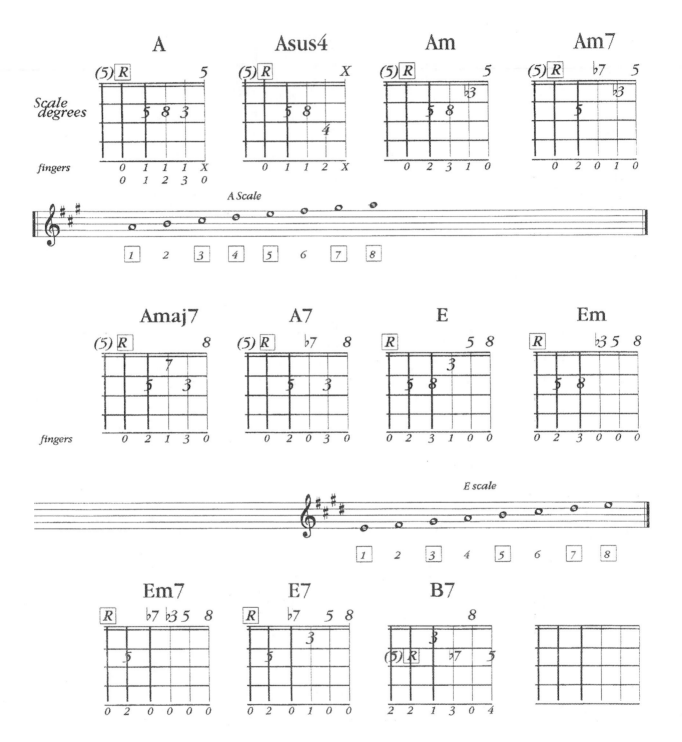

Quiz one: *Strum the following chords, once each.*

play:

G	C	G	D7	G	G7	C

C7	Fmaj7	Cmaj7	C	Am	D

Dsus4	D	Dmaj7	D7	G	D	Dm

Quiz two:

A	Asus4	A	A7	D	A	Am

Am7	A	Amaj7	A7	D	E

E7	A	E	Em	Em7	E	B7

E

Optional Exam: *Identify and write an harmonic analysis of the following chord progression. Identify the key, show chord functions and dominant resolution.*

CHAPTER TWO

> ### MOVABLE CHORD FORMS WITH ROOT ON THE ⑥ STRING

LESSON ONE: The F bar chord.

Movable chord forms do not usually use open strings. However, most originate from open string chords. The first group in this chapter originate from the open position (E) chord. The open strings are replaced by the first finger, which bars all six strings. This is one of the most valuable chord forms and even beginners should learn it as soon as possible. From this form it is possible to play almost any MAJOR, MINOR, DOMINANT 7, MINOR 7, MINOR 7(9), MINOR 7(13), DOMINANT 7(9), DOMINANT 7(13). First, we will concentrate on learning just the (F) major bar chord. EXERCISE ONE will use the I-IV-V-I progression in the key of [C]. At first, the (F) bar chord is difficult to master, but with patience and persistence, you will be rewarded. Be sure to keep your left thumb low and wrist out. Keep the bar (first) finger straight across the strings and let it overlap a little on top. NOTICE THE LOCATION OF THE 3RD SCALE DEGREE IN THE MOVABLE MAJOR BAR CHORD FORM. It is being played with the middle finger. The 3rd degree is a most important chord note. This note can be lowered to make a minor chord. For the improvisor and arranger, it is the strongest note in the chord.

When practicing any of these exercises, your first objective is to make the chord changes without hesitation. Later you can concentrate on getting more of the strings ringing clean. This is practiced by starting with the bass and playing down the strings one at a time slowly (the sound will go up).

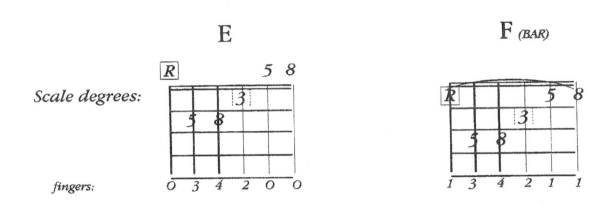

Quiz *Strum once for each chord.*

play: C   F   C   F   G7   C

Repeat until mastered.

LESSON TWO: *The fingerboard worksheet.*

To better prepare you for the next lessons, complete the following fingerboard worksheet. Play, write in the names, and notate only the natural notes one string at a time up to the 10th fret. Be especially careful with open string notation. Check yourself with the answer sheet in the back of the book.

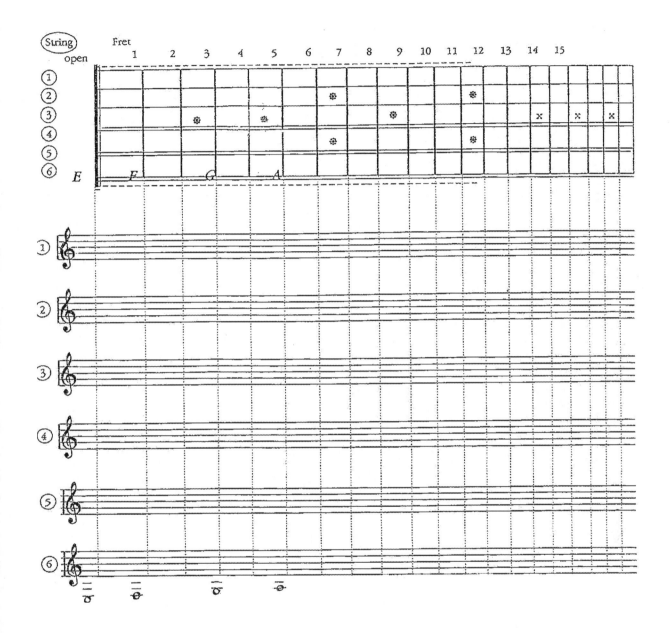

LESSON THREE: *Moving up the fingerboard with the movable MAJOR and MINOR bar chord forms with the root on the ⑥ string.*

CORRESPONDING SCALE FORM   Example: (G)   II position

Mastering the above scale form will help you better understand the chords in this chapter.

HOW TO STUDY THESE NEXT LESSONS:

Start with the open position (E) and move up the fingerboard playing the chords once each while saying the names. Lift your fingers off the strings each time. Notice that (E) and (F), (B) and (C) are only one fret apart (half steps). All other natural chords are two frets. Work your way up to the 10th fret (D) and then back down to open position (E). Do not play any sharp or flat chords at this time. Perform a random self quiz and then use the same system with the minor chords. Notice that the minor chords have the 3rd degree lowered (lift out the second finger). Use this system for each chord group.

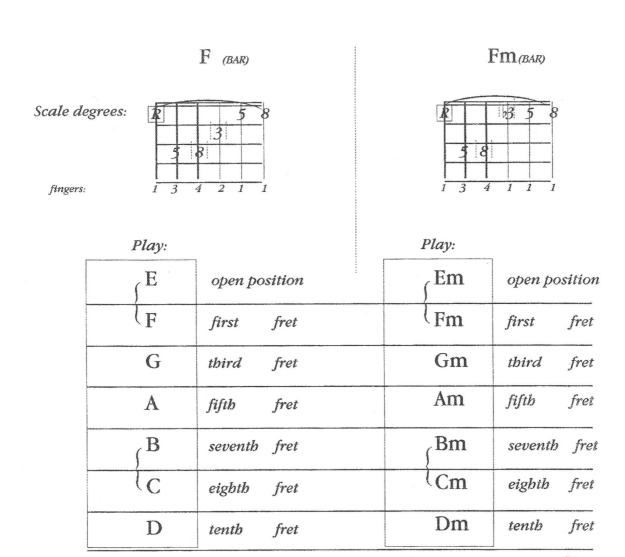

F (BAR)   Fm (BAR)

Scale degrees:

fingers: 1   3   4   2   1   1   1   3   4   1   1   1

Play:			Play:		
E	open position		Em	open position	
F	first	fret	Fm	first	fret
G	third	fret	Gm	third	fret
A	fifth	fret	Am	fifth	fret
B	seventh	fret	Bm	seventh	fret
C	eighth	fret	Cm	eighth	fret
D	tenth	fret	Dm	tenth	fret

Quiz

Play: C (8th fret)   Cm (flat the 3rd degree)   A

B♭   Am   Dm

* Memorize the location of the (8) degree. It is being played on the ④ th string with the 4th finger. In the next lesson, this chord note will be lowered two frets (♭7) to form the dominant 7th and minor 7th chords.

LESSON FOUR: The DOMINANT 7th and MINOR 7th forms with root on the ⑥ string.

These movable chord forms differ from the previous major and minor chords only by lowering the 8th degree two frets to a ♭7 (lift out the fourth finger). The 7th and 3rd degrees are the most important chord notes.

F 7

Scale degrees:

fingers: 1   3   1   2   1   1

F m 7

Scale degrees:

fingers: 1   3   1   1   1   1

Play:			Play:		
E7	open position		Em7	open position	
F7	first	fret	Fm7	first	fret
G7	third	fret	Gm7	third	fret
A7	fifth	fret	Am7	fifth	fret
B7	seventh	fret	Bm7	seventh	fret
C7	eighth	fret	Cm7	eighth	fret
D7	tenth	fret	Dm7	tenth	fret

Play:

C *(8th fret)*   C7 *(flat the (8) two frets)*

Cm7 *(flat the 3rd degree)*   A *(5th fret)*   Am

G   F   B♭   A   A7   Am7

G   Gm   Bm7*(7th fret)*   Cm7   Am7

Gm7 C   Cm

LESSON FIVE: An optional DOMINANT 7th form and an important MAJOR 7th built from it.

Unless you have a particular problem with bar chords, you may not find this following non-bar dominant 7th form as useful as the bar dominant 7th form. However, many other important movable chord forms are built from it.

Example: F7

Scale degrees:

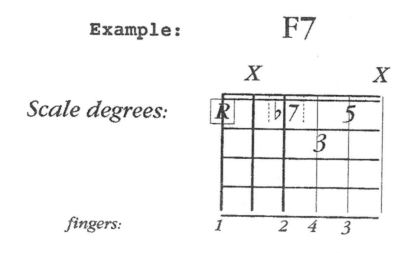

fingers: 1   2 4 3

The first of these new forms will be the MAJOR 7. This chord is often used in place of major chords where a richer sound is desirable. Notice that this form, along with the remaining two forms in this chapter, span only two frets.

Fmaj.7

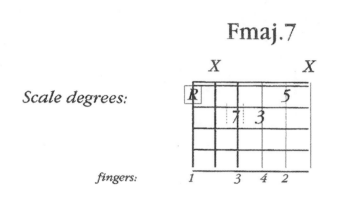

Scale degrees:

fingers: 1 3 4 2

Play:

Fmaj.7	first	fret
Gmaj.7	third	fret
Amaj.7	fifth	fret
Bmaj.7	seventh	fret
Cmaj.7	eighth	fret
Dmaj.7	tenth	fret

Quiz

Play: D maj.7   Amaj.7   B♭ maj.7   Gmaj.7   C

Cm   C   C7   Cm7   Cm   Cm7

LESSON SIX: The MINOR 7 (♭5) and the DIMINISHED 7th chord forms with the root on the ⑥ string.

Another name for the MINOR 7 (♭5), is HALF DIMINISHED (θ). It is made up of the Root (1), ♭3, ♭5, and ♭7 degrees. The DIMINISHED 7th is made up of the R, ♭3, ♭5, and diminished 7 (°7). It has a small bar. The only difference between these two chords is that the 7th degree is one fret lower on the diminished 7th. On both forms the root is being fretted with the second finger.

Example:

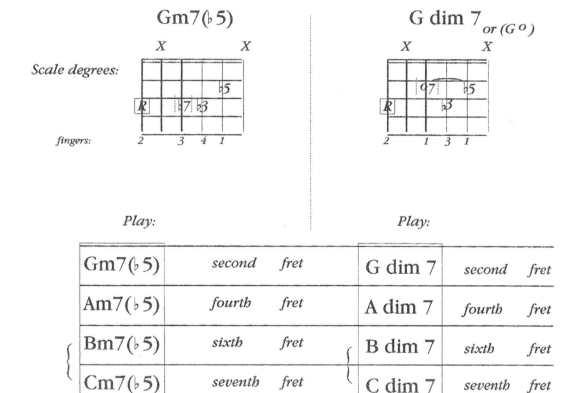

Gm7(♭5)	second	fret		G dim 7	second	fret
Am7(♭5)	fourth	fret		A dim 7	fourth	fret
Bm7(♭5)	sixth	fret		B dim 7	sixth	fret
Cm7(♭5)	seventh	fret		C dim 7	seventh	fret
Dm7(♭5)	nineth	fret		D dim 7	nineth	fret

LESSON SEVEN: More on DIMINISHED chords and the advancement exam.

Practice changing from MINOR 7 (♭5) to DIMINISHED 7. These two movable forms are used together often. However, it is much more common to name the diminished 7 as DOMINANT 7 (♭9) when it is preceded by the minor 7 (♭5). More on this in Chapter Three.

Any note in the diminished chord can be a root. That is why it repeats itself every three frets. Move a diminished 7 form up or down three frets and you will find the same notes. The easiest way to remember this will be to give priority to the position with the root on the ⑥ string.

Example:

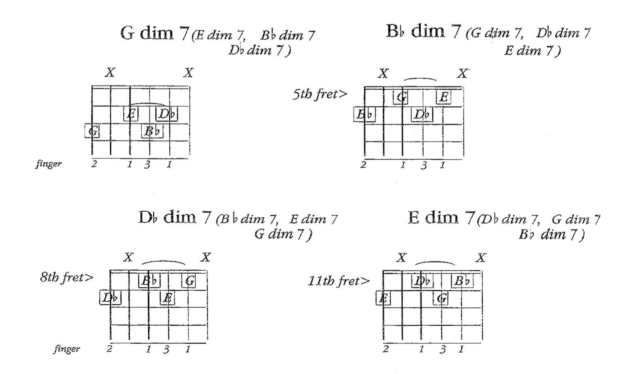

Play:

Dm7(♭5)   D dim 7 *(G7 ♭9)*   Am7(♭5)

A dim 7 *(D7 ♭9)*   Bm7(♭5)   B dim 7 *(E7 ♭9)*

G dim 7 *(2nd fret)*   B♭ dim 7 *(5th fret)*   D♭ dim 7

E dim 7 *(11th fret)*   Cm7(♭5)   C dim 7 *(F7 ♭9)*

Advancement Exam   *Don't forget that the fret position of a chord is determined by the finger farthest to the left.*

Play:

C *(8th fret)*   Cm *(♭3rd degree)*   Cm7 *(8th degree down to ♭7)*

C7 *(major 3rd)*   C   C♯ dim 7 *(8th fret)*

Dm7   G   G♯ dim 7   Am7   A

A7   Am7   Am7(♭5)   A dim 7

Cmaj7   Amaj7   B♭ maj7   Gmaj7

Am   G   F   E *(open pos.)*   Bm7(♭5)

B dim 7 *(E7 ♭9)*   Amaj7   Am7(♭5)

A dim 7 *(D7 ♭9)*   Gmaj7

CHAPTER THREE

MOVABLE CHORD FORMS WITH THE ROOT ON THE ⑤ STRING.

LESSON ONE: Moving up the fingerboard with the MAJOR and MINOR forms with the root on the ⑤ string.

These forms originate from the open position (A) chord. It is not absolutely necessary to bar all six strings, but be sure to at least get the root on the ⑤ string with the first finger. Be sure to keep your left thumb low and wrist out.

NOTICE THE POSITION OF THE 3rd DEGREE IN THE MAJOR FORM. It is being played with the fourth finger on the ② string. As we mentioned in CHAPTER TWO, the 3rd degree is a most important chord note. This is the note to be lowered to make a minor chord. Even for the improviser and arranger, it is the most important note in the chord.

CORRESPONDING SCALE FORM   Example: (C) II position

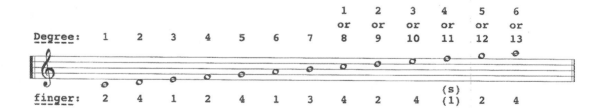

Mastering the above scale form will help you better understand the chords in this next chapter.

(s) = stretch

Use the same practicing method used for each lesson in CHAPTER TWO: Start with the open position forms and move up and down the fingerboard, strumming only the natural chords once each while saying the names. Lift your fingers off the strings each time. Notice the half steps between E and F, B and C.

Example:

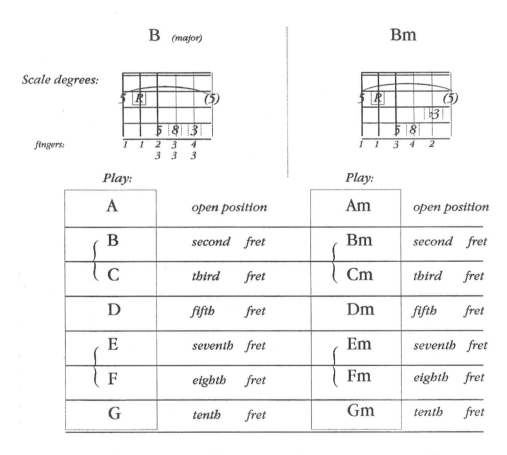

B (major)			Bm	
A	*open position*		Am	*open position*
B	*second fret*		Bm	*second fret*
C	*third fret*		Cm	*third fret*
D	*fifth fret*		Dm	*fifth fret*
E	*seventh fret*		Em	*seventh fret*
F	*eighth fret*		Fm	*eighth fret*
G	*tenth fret*		Gm	*tenth fret*

* Master the exercises on page 40 before proceeding to page 32.

Quiz

Play:

A   Am   D *(5th fret)*   Dm *(♭ 3rd)*   F

LESSON TWO: The DOMINANT 7 and MINOR 7 movable chord forms with the root on the ⑤ string.

These forms differ from the previous major and minor only by lowering the 8th degree (8va) two frets to a ♭ 7. The 7th and 3rd degrees are the most important chord notes.

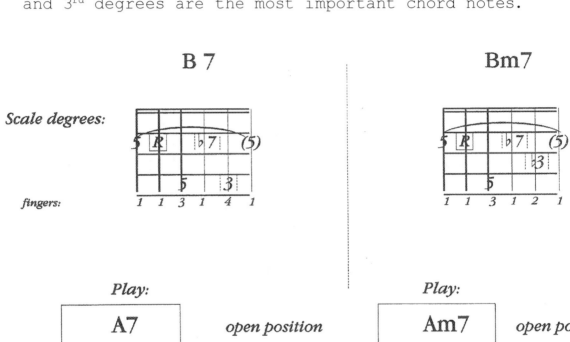

Play:		Play:	
A7	*open position*	Am7	*open position*
B7	*second fret*	Bm7	*second fret*
C7	*third fret*	Cm7	*third fret*
D7	*fifth fret*	Dm7	*fifth fret*
E7	*seventh fret*	Em7	*seventh fret*
F7	*eighth fret*	Fm7	*eighth fret*
G7	*tenth fret*	Gm7	*tenth fret*

Play :

F Fm (♭3) Fm7 (♭7) F7 (major 3)

C7 F7 C7 F7 C7 G7 F7

C7 (third fret) Gm Fm Em Em7

E♭ (sixth fret) E

LESSON THREE: The MAJOR 7 chord with the root on the ⑤ string.

MAJOR 7 chords are made up of the root (1), 3, 5, and 7 scale degrees. They have an entirely different character from the DOMINANT 7 which is made up of the root, 3, 5, and ♭7 degrees. MAJOR 7 chords usually function as I or IV chords within a key. The DOMINANT 7 chords usually function as a V chord, more on this in the next chapter.

Example:

Bmaj7

Scale degrees:

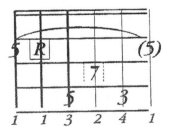

fingers: 1 1 3 2 4 1

Play:

Amaj.7	open position
Bmaj.7	second fret
Cmaj.7	third fret
Dmaj.7	fifth fret
Emaj.7	seventh fret
Fmaj.7	eighth fret
Gmaj.7	tenth fret

Quiz

Play: Cmaj 7   Fmaj 7   Dmaj 7 *(fifth fret)*   E♭maj 7

F   *(eighth fret)*   Fmaj 7   F7   Fm7 *(flat the 3rd degree)*

B♭   *(first fret)*   B♭maj 7   B♭7   *(flat the 8th two frets)*

B♭m 7   D   Dm   G   Gmaj 7   G7

Gm7   E♭   E♭maj 7   E♭7   E♭m 7

*Master the exercises on pages 41-
48 before advancing to page 35.*

LESSON FOUR: The MINOR 7 (♭5) and the DIMINISHED 7 forms with the root on the ⑤ string.

Notice that the third and fourth fingers do not move when changing back and forth between these two chord forms. Also notice that the DIMINISHED 7 form is the only form in this chapter wherein the root is not played with the first finger.

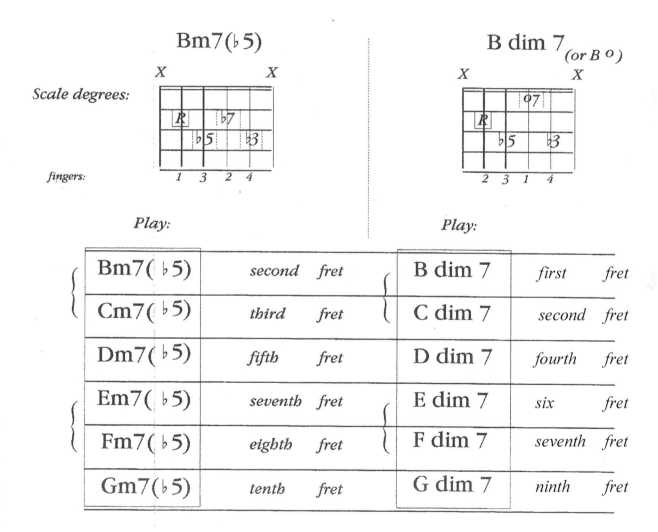

Bm7(♭5)	second	fret		B dim 7	first	fret
Cm7(♭5)	third	fret		C dim 7	second	fret
Dm7(♭5)	fifth	fret		D dim 7	fourth	fret
Em7(♭5)	seventh	fret		E dim 7	six	fret
Fm7(♭5)	eighth	fret		F dim 7	seventh	fret
Gm7(♭5)	tenth	fret		G dim 7	ninth	fret

LESSON FIVE: *The Dominant 7 (♭9) chord and the advancement exam.*

As we mentioned in CHAPTER TWO, practice changing back and forth from the MINOR 7 (♭ 5) to the DIMINISHED 7. The minor 7 (♭ 5) often functions as a (ii) chord within a minor key. It often preceeds a DOMINANT 7 (♭ 9), which is fingered exactly like the diminished 7. The DIMINISHED chord ("dim 7" or "dim" or ("°7") is often used as a chromatic passing chord such as (#i°) or a (♭ iii°). To better understand the dominant 7 (♭ 9), let's take a look at its constuction:

Example:

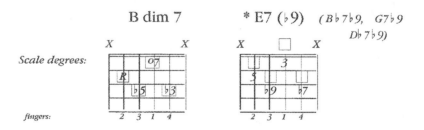

* You will notice the absence of a root in the DOMINANT 7 (♭ 9). The "assumed root" is any note one fret below a chord note. Like the DIMINISHED, this form repeats every three frets. See page 109 and 110 for an example.

Quiz

Play: Em7(♭5)   E dim 7 *(A7 ♭9)*   Cm7(♭5)

C dim 7*(F7 ♭9)*   Dmaj 7   D♯dim 7   Em7   F

Fmaj 7   F   Fm7   Fm7(♭5)   F dim 7 *(B ♭ 7 ♭9)*

E♭maj 7   E♭7   E♭m 7   E♭m 7(♭5)

E♭dim 7 *(A ♭ 7 ♭9)*

CHAPTER FOUR

> *Combining movable chord forms with the roots on the ⑤ and ⑥ strings.*

LESSON ONE: *Rhythms, and a review of movable chord forms.*

RHYTHMS:

You could make an interesting study of rhythms to strum chords. The important thing to remember is to keep your time steady and comfortable for other musicians to play along with. Keep your strumming simple and repetitious. The more common strums are also the most simple. Think of basic note values. Here are a few:

The quarter note strum: Use a down stroke on every beat.

The swing eighth note strum: Use a down stroke on the down beat and an up stroke on the up beat.

<u>REVIEW</u>:

This chapter will consist mainly of practical, typical example exercises for combining movable chord forms with the root on the ⑥ and ⑤ strings. Before we start however, let's review the movable forms covered so far and take a look at a few new ones.

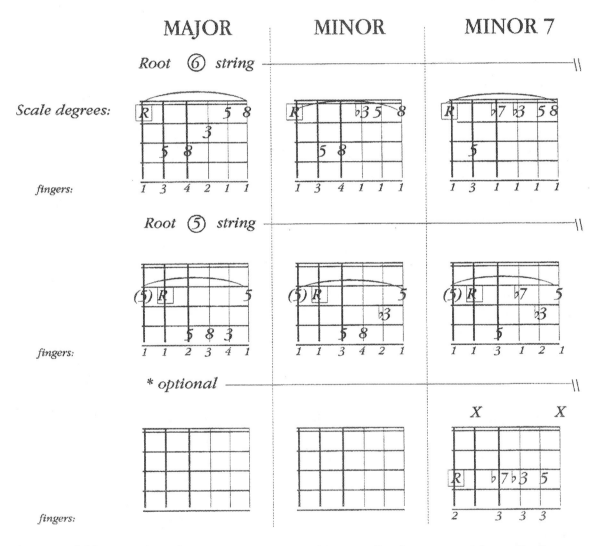

* We will study three note versions of these optional forms in upcoming lessons.

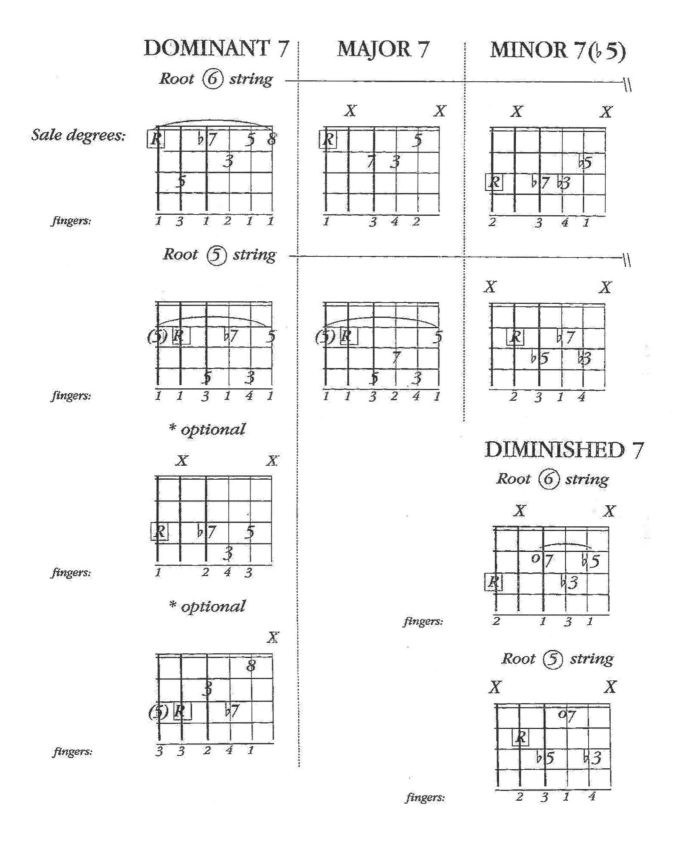

LESSON TWO: *Combining forms with the root on the ⑤ and ⑥ string.*

<u>EXERCISE ONE:</u> MAJOR CHORDS (triads - root, 3, 5, 8)

Play:

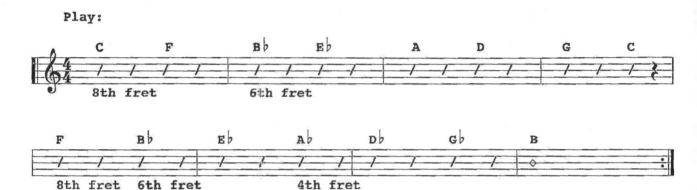

<u>EXERCISE TWO:</u> MINOR CHORDS (triads - root ♭3, 5, 8)

Play:

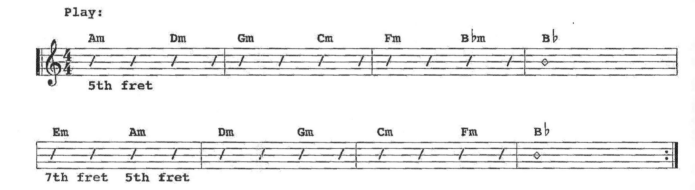

EXERCISE THREE: DOMINANT 7 chords (root, 3, *5*, ♭7, 8)

Play:

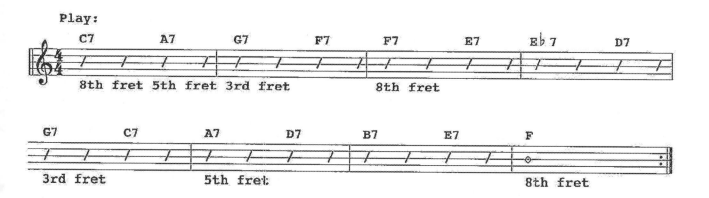

EXERCISE FOUR: Twelve bar blues in the key of [C].

Play:

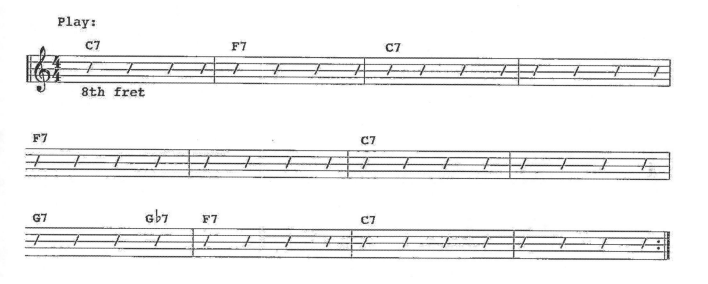

EXERCISE FIVE: Eight bar blues in the key of [G].

Play:

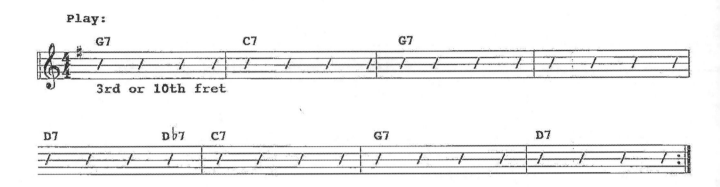

3rd or 10th fret

EXERCISE SIX: ten bar blues in the key of [A].

Play:

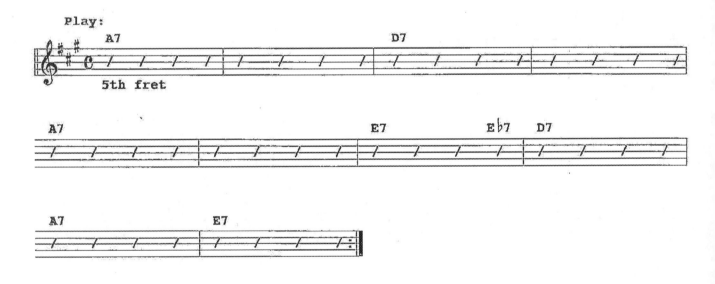

5th fret

Play:

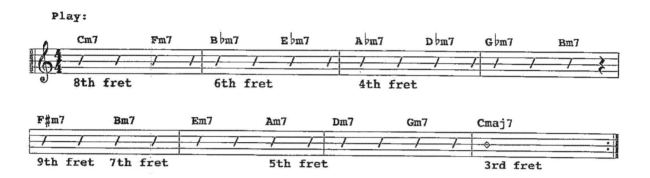

LESSON THREE: *More chord exercises.*

EXERCISE ONE: The I - IV - V - I chord progression with
movable forms.

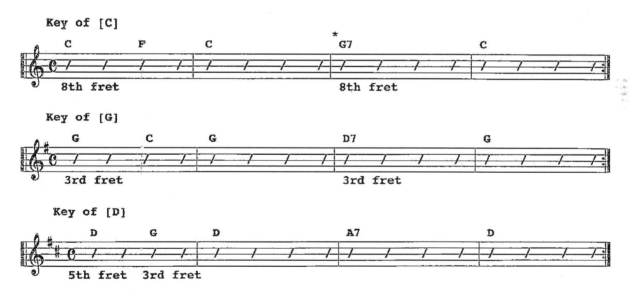

* Refer to the bottom of page 39 for this form.

EXERCISE TWO: The I - vi - IV - V - I chord progression
with movable forms.

Key of [C]

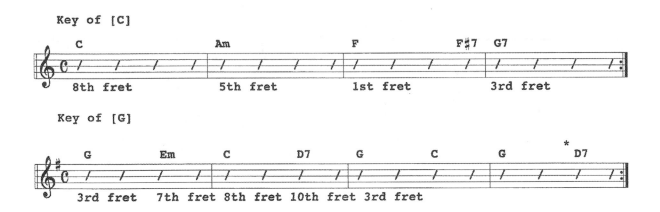

Key of [G]

EXERCISE THREE: "STORMY MONDAY BLUES" twelve bar blues

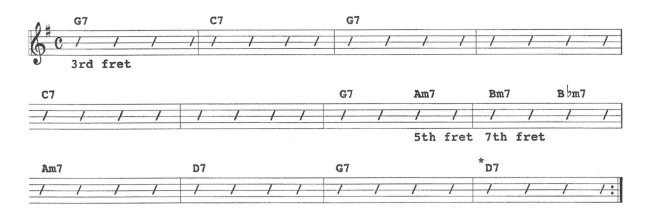

* As an optional ear training exercise, make a recording
of EXERCISE ONE and TWO. On playback, identify the chord
function (i.e. I IV vi etc.) without looking at the book. As
a more advanced exercise, do the same with EXERCISES FOUR
and FIVE after you have performed the harmonic analysis.

* Use the optional form found on the bottom of page 39.

EXERCISE FOUR: Chord progressions with secondary dominant
                7 chords.

Key of [A]

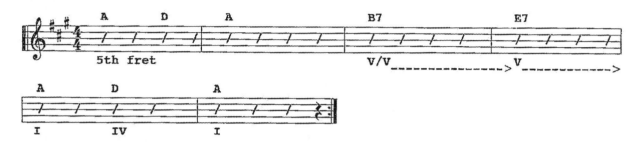

Key of [E]

EXERCISE FIVE: Chord progressions using secondary dominants,
                extended dominants and the iv minor chord.
                Identify the keys.

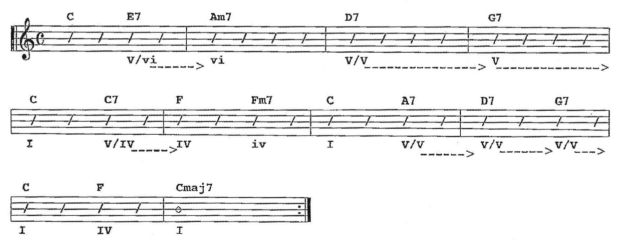

        This progression is in the key of _____ .

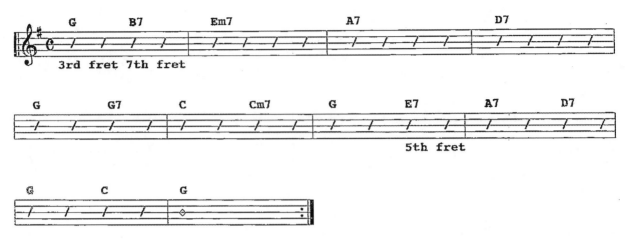

3rd fret 7th fret

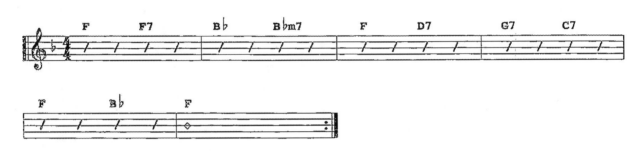

5th fret

This progression is in the key of _____.

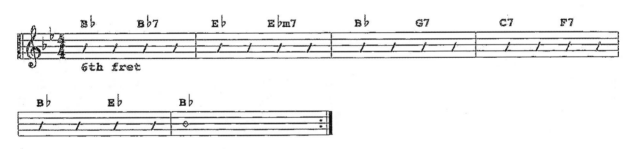

This progression is in the key of _____.

6th fret

This progression is in the key of _____.

*As an optional music theory assignment, do an harmonic analysis of the chord progressions on this page.

EXERCISE SIX: A ii - v chord progression exercise.

Play:

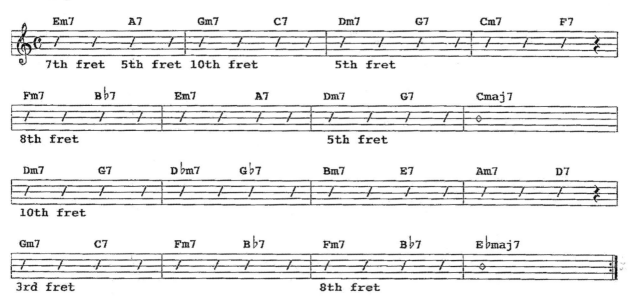

LESSON FOUR:

EXERCISE ONE: MAJOR 7 chords (root, 3, 5, 7, 8)

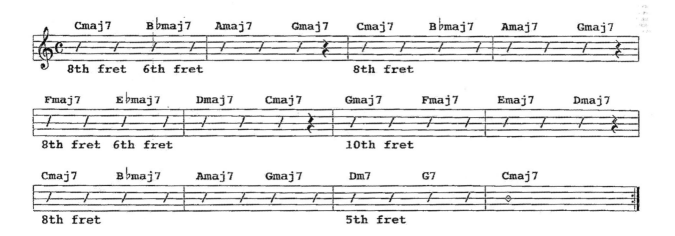

EXERCISE TWO:

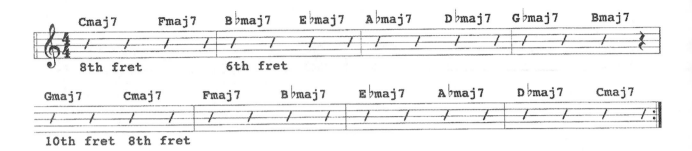

EXERCISE THREE: The ii - V - I chord progression. This chord combination is often used in jazz for modulations or temporary key changes.

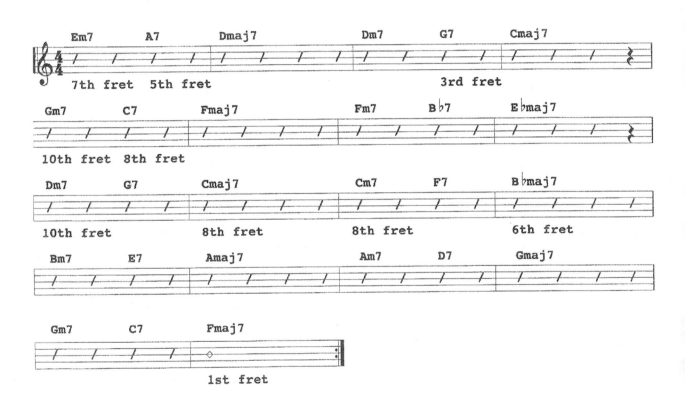

EXERCISE FOUR: The DIMINISHED 7 chord (R, ♭3, ♭5, °7) This
exercise uses diminished (dim.) forms with
the root on the ⑥ string. Be sure to start
on the 3rd fret.

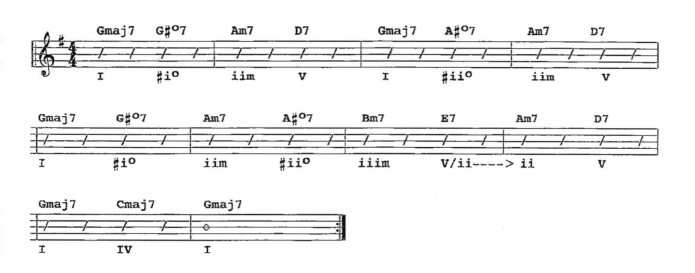

EXERCISE FIVE: This exercise uses diminished forms with the
root on the ⑤ string. Start on the 3rd fret.

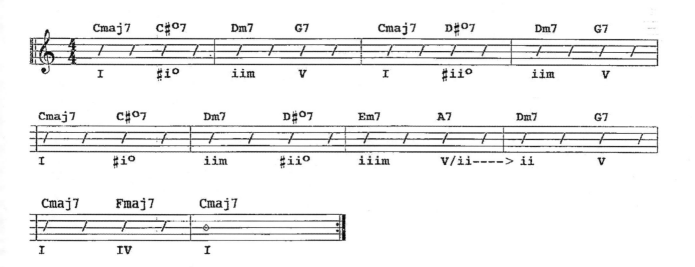

EXERCISE SIX: The MINOR 7 (♭5) chord (R, ♭3, ♭5, ♭7).

EXERCISE SEVEN: This exercise starts with the minor 7 (♭5) form with the root on the ⑥ string. Measure five uses the form with the root on the ⑤ string.

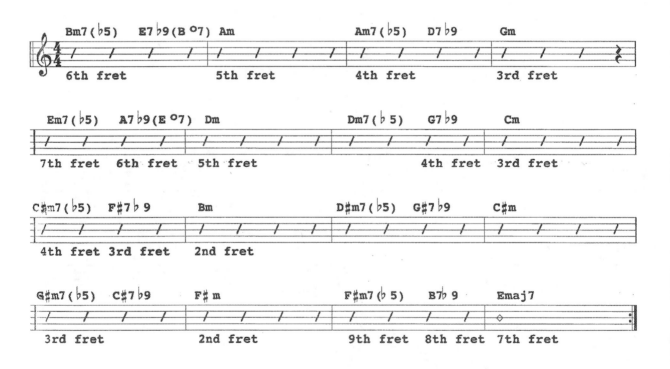

* Remember: Chord fret position is determined by the finger farthest to the left.

CHAPTER FIVE

Advanced Studies

> *NINTH, THIRTEENTH, and SIXTH chords,*
> *SUBSTITUTE DOMINANTS, SMALL*
> *FORMS and THREE NOTE FORMS.*

MAJOR 6, MAJOR 7, MAJOR 6(9) and MAJOR 7 $\frac{(9)}{(13)}$ chords can be used as substitutes for each other or for MAJOR (triad) chords when a richer "jazzier" sound is desired. Care should be taken with the MAJOR 6/9 and the MAJOR 7 $\frac{(9)}{(13)}$. These chords are extremely rich and sometimes can be used only as ending chords in many musical styles. MAJOR chords, on the other hand, can be used as substitutes for any of the above mentioned chords. Another situation for caution is when the melody has a strong first scale degree. In this case the rhythm instrument playing a chord with a major 7 degree may clash. MAJOR 6, MAJOR 6 (9) or a MAJOR chord with the 3rd degree in the bass (1st inversion) may be a better choice here if a richer sound than the root position major chord is desired.

MINOR 7, MINOR 6, MINOR 7(9) and MINOR 7 $\frac{(9)}{(13)}$ chords can be used as substitutes for each other and often as substitutes for the MINOR (triad).

There are many substitutions for the DOMINANT 7 chords. The most readily useful are the DOMINANT 9 and the DOMINANT 13. Both of these chords are called dominant because they have a ♭7 degree. 13 chords usually have a 9th degree but not always. The 13th and 6th degrees are the same note. The chord is referred to as a (13) chord if the ♭7 is present. It is a (6) chord if the ♭7 is not present. <u>ALTERED DOMINANT</u> chords, (any combination of ♯5, ♭5, ♯9 and ♭9) can be substituted for DOM.7, especially as embellishments or in "turnarounds". Altered degrees can be interchangeable. For example; if a tune calls for a C7♭9, in addition or in place of the ♭9, you could also possibly play C7♯9, C7$^{(♭9)}_{(♯5)}$, C7$^{(♭9)}_{(♭5)}$, C7$^{(♯9)}_{(♭5)}$, or C7$^{(♯9)}_{(♯5)}$ Plain DOM.7 chords can be used as a conservative substitute for DOM.9, DOM.13 and often for the ALTERED chords.

LESSON ONE: *Adding the 9th and (or) 13th degrees to the optional MINOR 7 and DOMINANT 7 chord forms.*

Try this MINOR 7 chord form

Instead of this MINOR 7

Scale degrees:

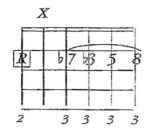

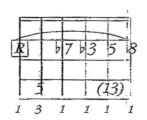

fingers:

So that you can get to this

*DOMINANT 7(9)

Instead of this DOMINANT 7

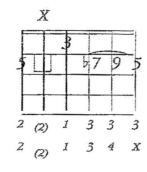

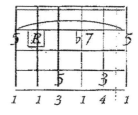

fingers:

* This movable form originates from the optional dominant 7 with the root on the ⑤ string (page 39). The second finger can be placed on either the ⑤ or ⑥ string or both.

EXERCISE ONE: The ii - V - I chord exercise using the optional minor 7 chord with the root on the ⑥ string and the DOMINANT 7(9) with the root or the assumed root on the ⑤ string.

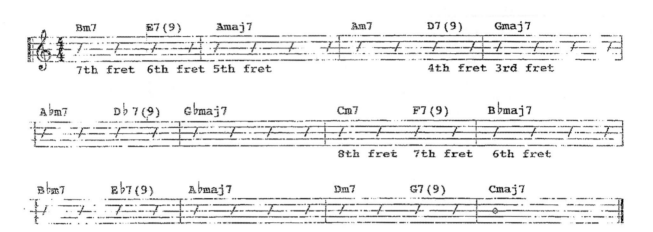

EXERCISE TWO: A good way to embellish these last chord forms is to add the 9th degree to the MINOR 7 chord and the 13th degree to the DOM. 7(9) chord. Practice EXERCISE ONE again, this time add the fourth finger to the first beat of each of those chords. Lift the fourth finger on the second beat of each chord.

Example:

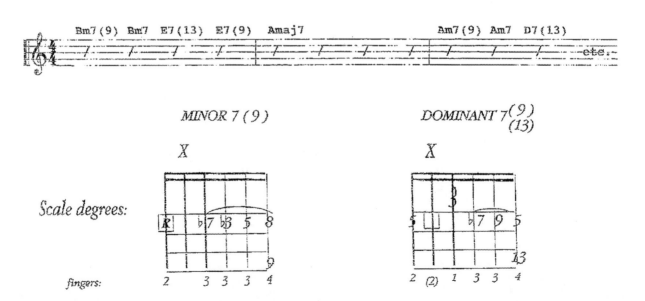

LESSON TWO: Adding the 9th and 13th degrees to the optional MINOR 7 chord with the root on the ⑤ string and the optional DOMINANT 7 with the root on the ⑥ string.

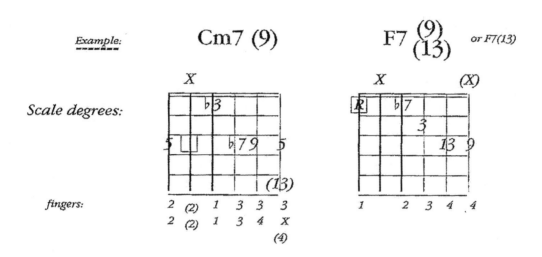

EXERCISE ONE: ii - V - I using the new forms.

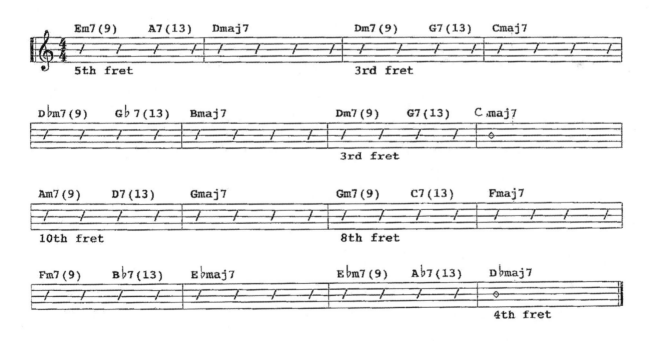

HERE ARE SOME OTHER VERY USEFUL FORMS THAT ARE BUILT FROM THE OPTIONAL DOMINANT 7 WITH THE ROOT ON THE ⑤ STRING, USING (C) FOR EXAMPLE:

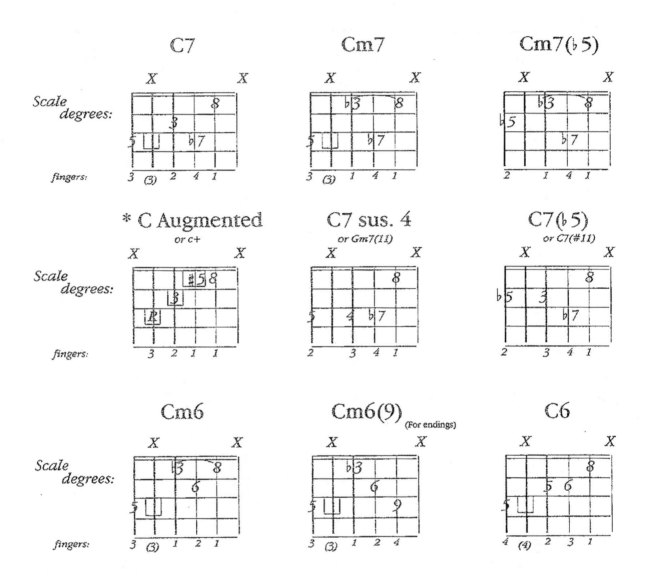

*This is the AUGMENTED triad. Augmented means #5. Like the DIMINISHED 7 chord, any note can be considered a root and it repeats itself every four frets. The above (C+) can also be a E+ or a G#+, every four frets.

LESSON THREE: The MAJOR 6 (9) chord with the root on the ⑤ string, the MAJOR 6 and the MAJOR 7 $^{(9)}_{(13)}$ chords with the root on the ⑥ string.

EXERCISE ONE: Go back to EXERCISE ONE of the previous lesson. Practice it again, but replace the major 7 chord with the MAJOR 6(9). This is a great substitute when a richer, more exotic sound is desired. Be sure to play the new chord on the correct fret.

Example: # C 6 (9)

Scale degrees:

fingers:

EXERCISE TWO: Practice the same exercise, this time strumming the MAJOR 7 chord on the first two beats of the measure and then the MAJOR 6(9) on the last two.

EXERCISE THREE: Go back to page 54 and practice EXERCISE ONE with the MAJOR 6 chord replacing the MAJOR 7. The MAJOR 6 chord will be one fret lower than the MAJOR 7.

Example:

G6

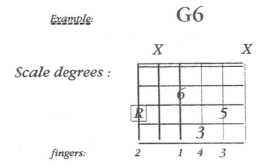

EXERCISE FOUR: Use the same page 54 exercise. This time strum the MAJOR 7 on the first two beats of the measure and then the MAJOR 6 on the last two.

EXERCISE FIVE: The MAJOR 7 $^{(9)}_{(13)}$ chord. This is an extremely rich substitute for the MAJOR 7 chord. It is also used effectively for endings.

Example:

Gmaj 7 $^{(9)}_{(13)}$ *or Gmaj7(13)*

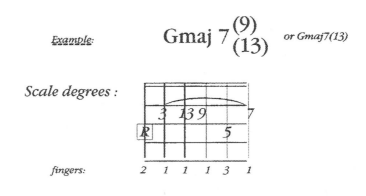

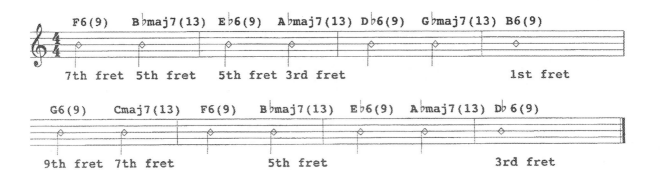

HERE ARE SOME OTHER VERY USEFUL FORMS THAT ARE BUILT FROM THE OPTIONAL DOMINANT 7 WITH THE ROOT ON THE ⑥ STRING.

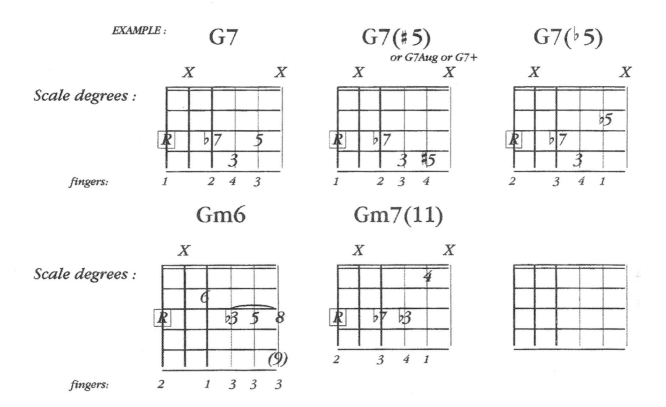

LESSON FOUR: *The SUBSTITUTE DOMINANT.*

DOMINANT 7 chords with the same tritone (i.e. the same 3rd and ♭7th) can be substituted for each other. In the example you will notice that the 3rd and ♭7 in the (G7) chord are also the 3rd and ♭7 in the (D♭7). The order however, is reversed.

EXERCISE ONE: Let's put this concept to practical use. In the exercise from page 54, use the SUBSTITUTE DOMINANT in place of the DOMINANT 7(9). Use this DOMINANT 7(13) form for the sub:

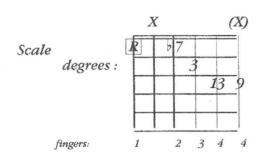

THE ORIGINAL EXERCISE

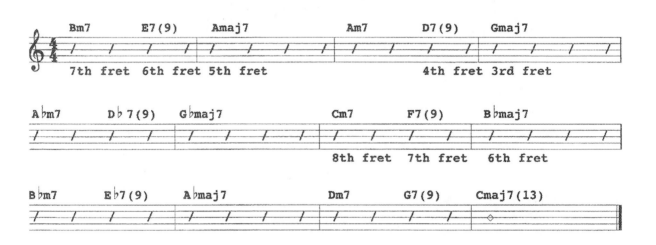

THE SAME EXERCISE USING THE SUBSTITUTE DOMINANT:

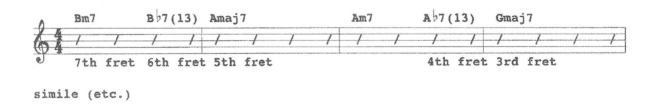

simile (etc.)

EXERCISE TWO: Apply the same instructions to the exercise from page 55. Use the SUBSTITUTE DOMINANT in place of the DOMINANT 7(13) chord. Use this DOMINANT 7(9) for the sub:

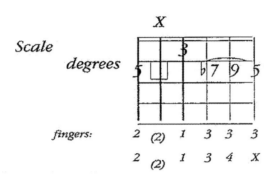

THE ORIGINAL EXERCISE

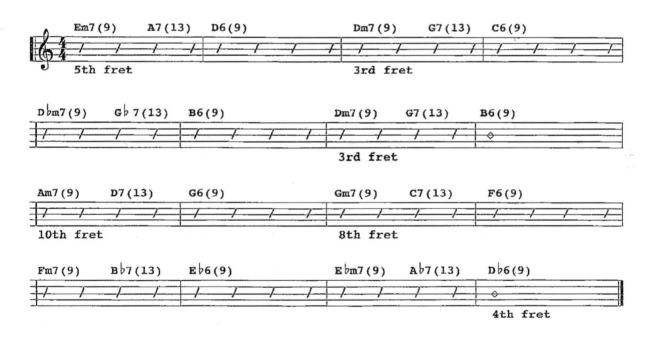

THE SAME EXERCISE USING THE SUBSTITUTE DOMINANT:

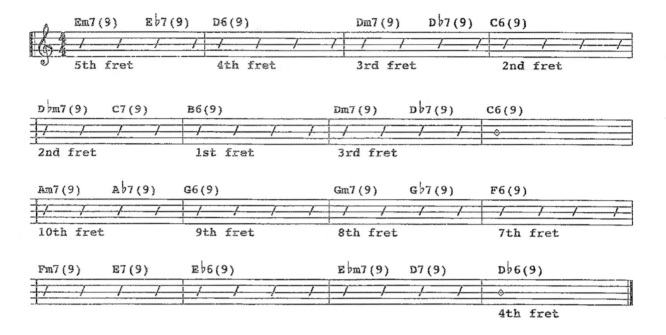

There are other ways to use the Substitute Dominants, such as using both the original and the sub. For example: play the original on the first beat or beats and the sub. on the next beats. Or switch them around; play the sub on first beats and the original on the next beats.

LESSON FIVE: *Review and a few new movable chord forms.*

The exercises in this lesson will be a little more challenging than previous exercises. They will be more like real jazz tunes.

EXERCISE ONE:

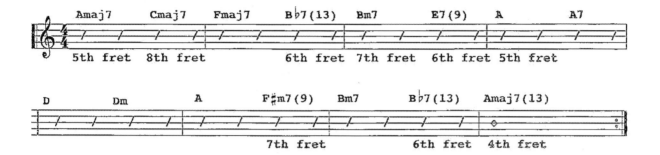

EXERCISE TWO: Some 6 chords.

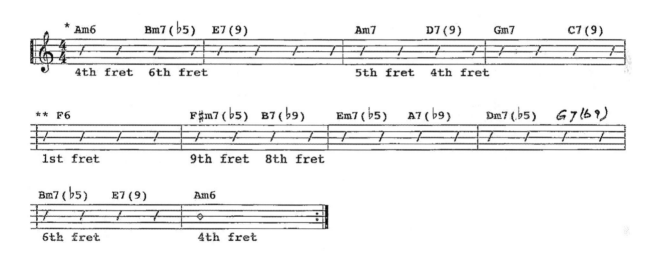

* (6) chords are good substitutions for triads or vice versa. This MINOR 6 chord, with the root on the ⑥ string is from page 59 and yes, it is the same finger formation as the dominant 7 with the root on the ⑤ string.

** This new movable form is built from the first major with the root on the ostring. Notice that the ④ string is deadened. If it is sounded, the ♭7 degree would make the chord a dom. 7(13). See the next page for the diagram.

F 6

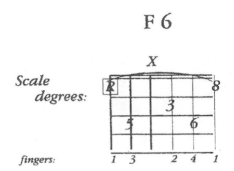

Scale degrees:

fingers:

EXERCISE THREE: AUGMENTED triads

(R,3,#5) This movable form where any finger can be a root can be found on page 56. It is a good sub for +7

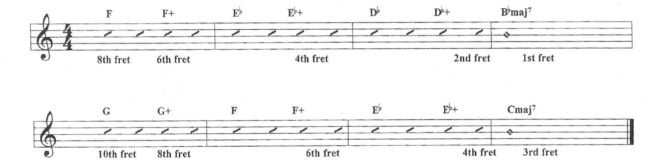

EXERCISE FOUR: AUGMENTED 7 (R,3, #5, ♭7) This movable chord with the root on the ⑥ string can be found on page 59.

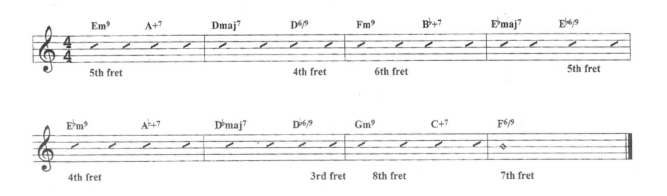

LESSON SIX: Minor chord sequences.

Minor chord sequences are used to put movement and interest into long and monotonous minor chord duration. They can be performed by starting with a minor chord form and then lowering the 8va or root one fret at a time. The following examples use the first movable forms studied in this method: The form with the root on the ⑥ string and the form with the root on the ⑤ string.

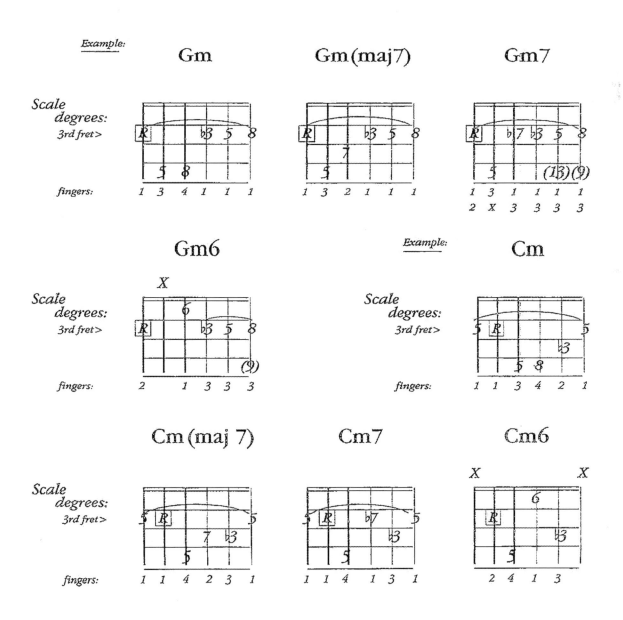

<u>EXERCISE ONE:</u>

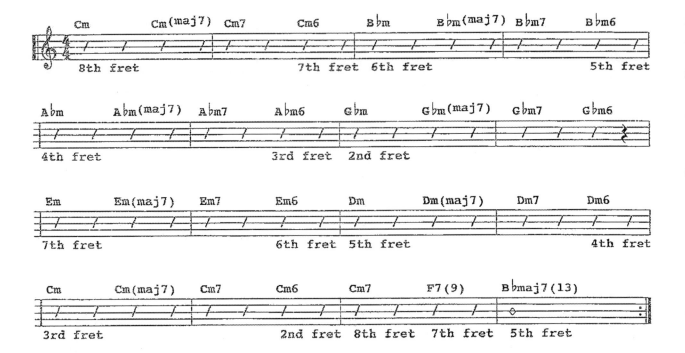

Another minor chord sequence can be played by starting with a minor triad and then raising the 5th degree one fret at a time. For this example we will use a movable three note form with the root on the ⑥ string.

<u>Example:</u>

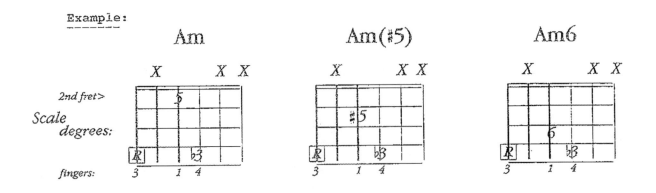

EXERCISE TWO:

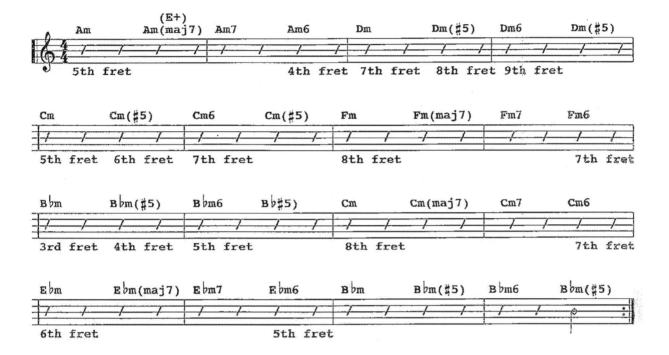

LESSON SEVEN: *Chords with notes other than the root in the bass.*

We often see chord symbols requesting different chord or scale degrees in the bass. EXAMPLE: C7/B♭ Dm7/C B♭/C Am7/C etc. Most but not all of these are inversions (chord degrees other than the root in the bass, see page 12). You can ignore these special requests and play only what is written to the left of the slash. However, it is often more fun and challenging to play the inversion or to improvize your own harmonized bass lines. More on this fascinating concept in the next lesson.

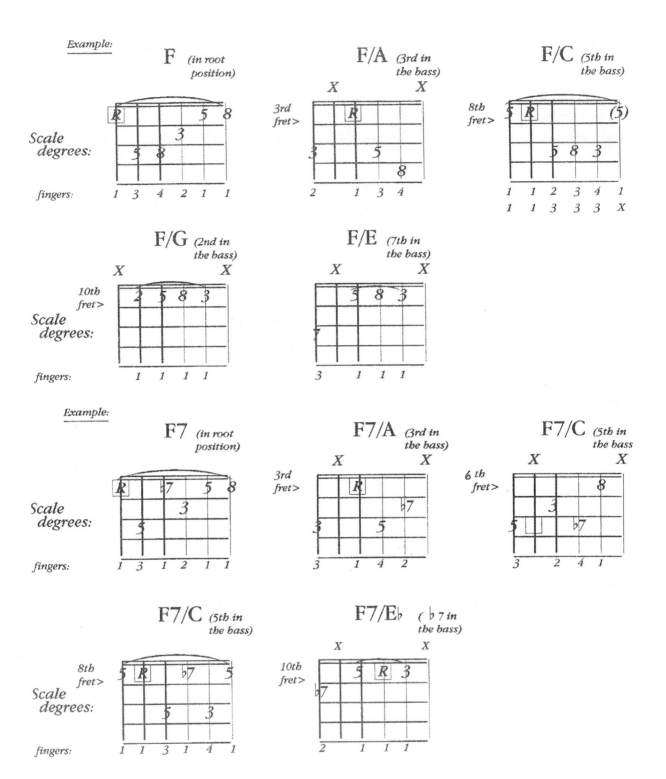

Example:

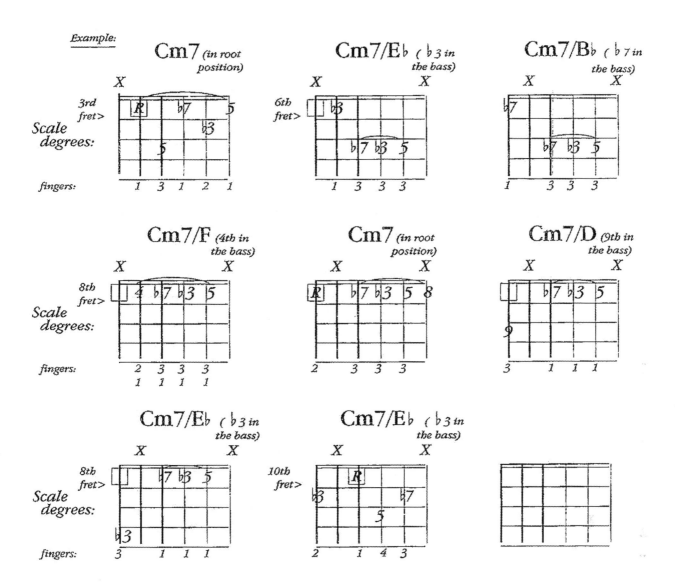

EXERCISE: Practice these chord sequences in order, one strum each until you can make the changes without hesitation.

CHAPTER SIX   Advanced Studies

> *MOVABLE THREE NOTE CHORD FORMS, HARMONIZED BASS LINES and ALTERED DOMINANT CHORDS.*

LESSON ONE: *Harmonized bass lines with three note DOMINANT 7 chords.*

In active chording, such as harmonized bass lines, you will be able to move faster and cleaner with three note forms as opposed to full chord forms. Harmonized bass lines are used along with embellished full and partial chord forms for a solid rhythm or as a comping technique. In other words, they are used as an important element of creative, interesting, varied accompaniment. In addition to the obvious benefit for all guitarists, this concept is especially useful for those who for one reason or another, find full forms impractical. The strongest of these have the root or 5th degree in the bass (root position or second inversion). When you start a bass line at the chord change, start with one of these. They have the 3rd and 7th degree (the others may not have both) and are better used in passing from one strong chord to another. Practice playing these forms in sequence until you feel you have mastered the movement. Start with the root position, play one strum each up to G7/F and then backtrack down to G7. On the right hand you can use either pick or finger style. If the latter is applied use the thumb, index and middle finger (p, i and m).

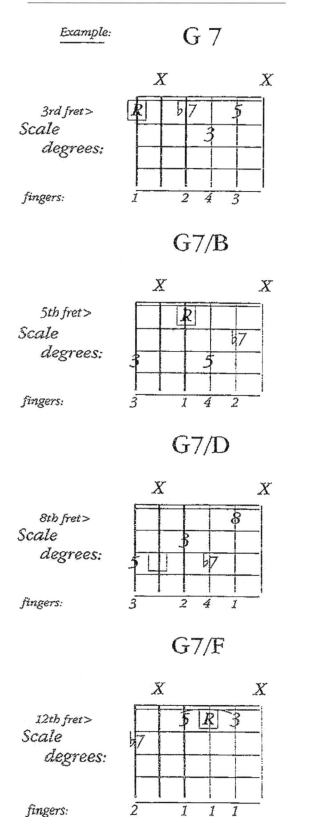

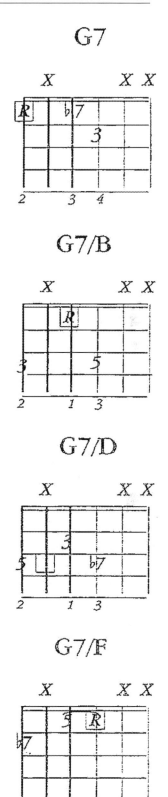

In the following exercises, using G BLUES for example, you will see some of the many interesting ways of improvising harmonized bass lines using the four new three note movable chord forms. Practice these exercises extensively. They must be completely mastered.

EXERCISE ONE:

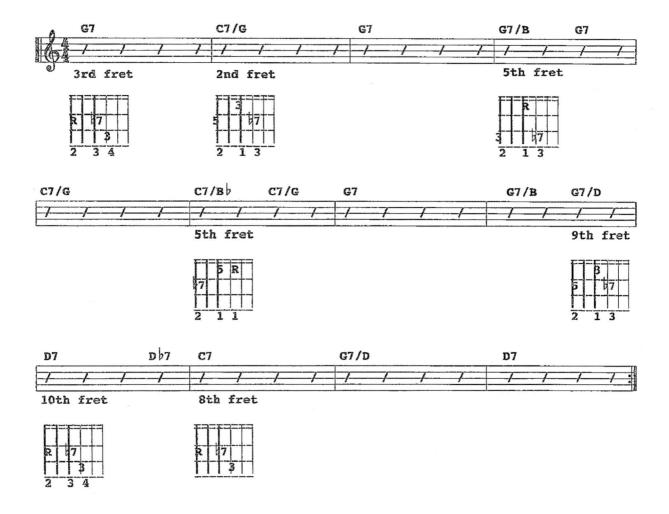

EXERCISE TWO:

G7	G7/B	G7/D	G7/F	C7	C7/E	C7	C7/Bb

3rd fret   5th fret 9th fret 12th fret 8th fret 10th fret 8th fret 5th fret

G7	G7/B	G7/D	G7/F	G7/D	G7/B	G7	G7/B

3rd fret   5th fret   9th fret 12th fret 9th fret   5th fret   3rd fret 5th fret

C7	C7/Bb	C7	C7/E	C7/G	C7/E	C7	C7/Bb

2nd fret   5th fret   8th fret 10th fret 14th fret 10th fret   8th fret 5th fret

G7	G7/B	G7/D	G7/B	G7	G7/B	G7/D	G7/B

3rd fret   5th fret   9th fret   5th fret

D7/A	D7/C	D7	D7/C	C7/G	C7/Bb	C7/G	C7/Bb

4th fret   7th fret 10th fret   2nd fret   5th fret

G7	G7/B	G7/D	G7/B	G7/D	G7/B	G7

3rd fret   5th fret

EXERCISE THREE:

Practice EXERCISE TWO again. This time play one fret <u>below</u> or <u>above</u> the target chord on the first beat of the change. Then slide to the target fret on the next beat. Practice the remaining exercises in the lesson using this technique.

Example:

EXERCISE FOUR:

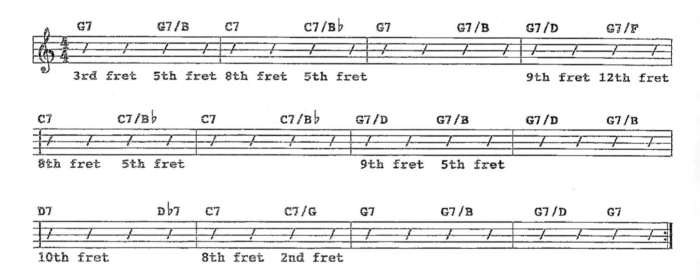

LESSON TWO: Harmonized bass lines for MAJOR 7 chords using three note forms and elements of the harmonized scale with bass movement on the ⑥ string.

<u>THE ORIGINAL COMPLETE FORM</u>   <u>THE NEW THREE NOTE FORM</u>

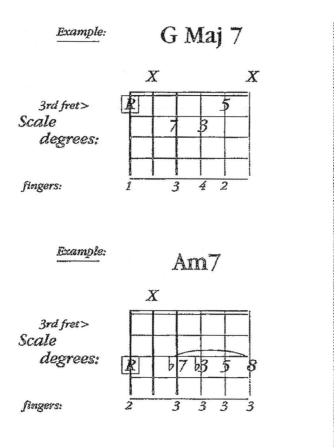 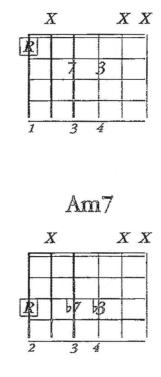

Example:

G Maj 7   **G Maj 7**

Am7   **Am7**

3rd fret> Scale degrees:

fingers:

Example:

3rd fret> Scale degrees:

fingers:

EXERCISE ONE: The chord symbol on top will exemplify what you will see written in a tune. The chords underneath that symbol are a suggested harmonized bass line.

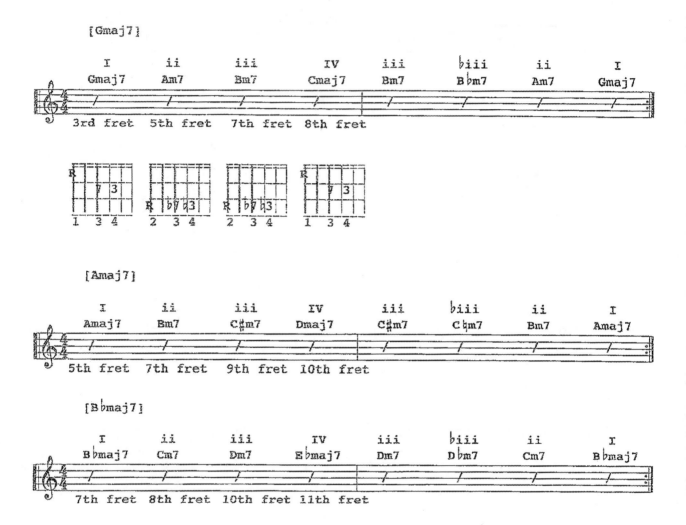

Feel free to experiment with different patterns. For example, start on the [I] chord then jump up to the [IV] chord and work down. Another would be to start on the [I] chord, go up to the [iii] then up to the [IV] chord then down to the [ii].

EXERCISE TWO: Combining MAJOR 7 and DOMINANT 7 harmonized
bass lines.

[Gmaj7]   [Cmaj7]

Gmaj7   Am7   B♭m7   Bm7   Cmaj7   Em7   Dm7   Cmaj7

3rd fret 5th fret 6th fret 7th fret 8th fret 12th fret 10th fret

[Gmaj7]   [G7]

Gmaj7   Bm7   B♭m7   Am7   G7   G7/B

3rd fret 7th fret 6th fret 5th fret 3rd fret   5th fret

[C7]

C7   B7/D♯   C7/E   B7/F♯   C7/G   C7

8th fret 9th fret 10th fret 13th fret 14th fret   8th fret

[G7]

G7   G♭7/B♭   G7/B   G♭7/D♭   G7/D   G7/B   G7

3rd fret 4th fret 5th fret 8th fret 9th fret   5th fret 3rd fret

[D7]   [C7]

D7/A   D7/C   D7   D7/C   C7/G   C7/B♭   C7   C7/B♭

4th fret 7th fret 10th fret

[G7]   [D7]

G7   G♭7/B♭   G7/B   D♭7   D7   D7/C   D7/A

LESSON THREE: *Harmonized bass lines for MINOR 7 chords with bass movement on the ⑥ string.*

THE ORIGINAL COMPLETE FORM

THE NEW THREE NOTE FORM

Example:

Gm7

X   X

3rd fret >
Scale degrees:

R   ♭7 ♭3   5

fingers: 2   3 3 3

Gm7

X   X X

R   ♭7 ♭3

fingers: 2   3 4

Gm7/B♭

X   X

5th fret >
Scale degrees:

♭3   R   ♭7
        5

fingers: 2   1   4   3

Gm7/B♭

X   X X

♭3   R
        5

fingers: 2   1   4

Gm7/D

X   X

8th fret >
Scale degrees:

     ♭3   8
5   ♭7

fingers: 3   1   4   1

Gm7/D

X   X X

     ♭3
5   ♭7

fingers: 3   1   4

EXERCISE ONE:

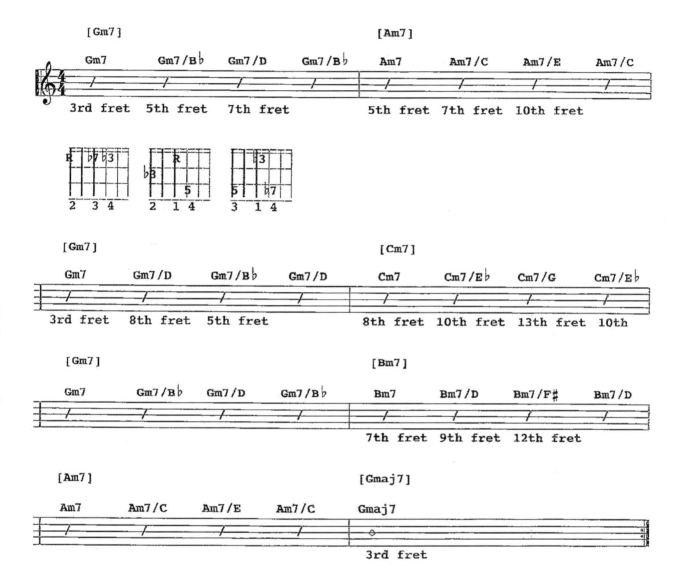

EXERCISE TWO: Combining MAJOR 7, MINOR 7 and DOMINANT 7
bass lines.

[Gmaj7]

Gmaj7	Am7	B♭m7	Bm7	Cmaj7	Bm7	B♭m7

3rd fret 5th fret 6th fret 7th fret 8th fret

[Am7]   [D7]

Am7	Am7/C	Am7/E	Am7/C	D7	D7/C	D7/A	D7/F♯

5th fret 7th fret 10th fret   10th fret 7th fret 4th fret 2nd fret

[Gmaj7]

Gmaj7	Cmaj7	Bm7	Am7	Gmaj7	Am7	B♭m7

3rd fret 8th fret 7th fret 5th fret

[Bm7]   [E7]

Bm7	Bm7/D	Bm7/F♯	Bm7/D	E7	E7/D	E7/B	E7/G♯

7th fret 9th fret 12th fret   12th fret 9th fret 6th fret 2nd fret

[Am7]   [D7]

Am7	Am7/C	Am7/E	Am7/C	D7	D7/C	D7/A	D7/F♯

10th fret 7th fret 4th fret 2nd fret

[Gmaj7]   [Cmaj7]   [Gmaj7]

Gmaj7	Am7	Cmaj7	G♯maj7	Gmaj7

LESSON FOUR: Harmonized bass lines for the MAJOR 7 chord using elements of the harmonized scale with bass movement on the ⑤ string.

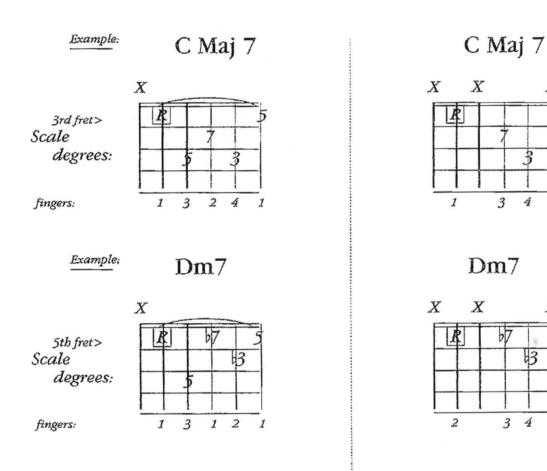

THE ORIGINAL COMPLETE FORM   *THE NEW THREE NOTE FORM*

EXERCISE ONE:

[Cmaj7]

| Cmaj7 | Dm7 | E♭m7 | Em7 | Fmaj7 | Em7 | Dm7 | Cmaj7 |

3rd fret   5th fret   6th fret   7th fret   8th fret

[Fmaj7]

| Fmaj7 | Gm7 | A♭m7 | Am7 | B♭maj7 | Am7 | Gm7 | Fmaj7 |

8th fret   10th fret   11th fret   12th fret   13th fret

[Cmaj7]

| Cmaj7 | Fmaj7 | Em7 | E♭m7 | Dm7 | Cmaj7 | Bmaj7 | Cmaj7 |

3rd fret

[E♭maj7]

| E♭maj7 | Fm7 | G♭m7 | Gm7 | A♭maj7 | Gm7 | Fm7 | E♭maj7 |

6th fret   8th fret   9th fret   10th fret   11th fret

* In the next exercise you will use this optional MAJOR 7/5:

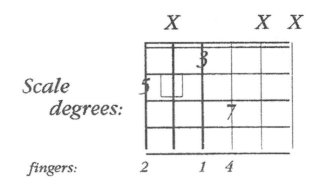

Scale degrees:

fingers: 2   1 4

EXERCISE TWO: Harmonized bass lines with bass movement on the ⑥ strings and ⑤ strings.

[Cmaj7]   [Dm7]   [G7]

Cmaj7   Dm7   E♭m7   Em7   Dm7   Dm7/F   G7/F   G7/D

8th fret   10th fret 11th fret 12th fret 10th fret 12th fret 12th fret

[Cmaj7]   [C7]

Cmaj7   Dm7   E♭m7   Em7   C7/G   C7/E   C7   C7/B♭

                                            14th fret 10th fret 8th fret 5th

[Fmaj7]

Fmaj7   B♭maj7   Am7   Gm7   Fmaj7   B♭maj7   Am7   Gm7

8th fret   13th fret 12th fret 10th fret

[Cmaj7]

                                    *
Cmaj7   Em7/B   Dm7/A   Cmaj7/B   Cmaj7   Dm7   E♭m7   Em7

8th fret   5th fret   3rd fret   2nd fret   3rd fret

[G7]   [F7]

G7/D   G7/F   G7/D   G7/B   F7/C   F7/E♭   F7/C   F7/A

8th fret   12th fret   5th fret   7th fret   10th fret   3rd fret

[Cmaj7]   [G7]   [C6/9]

Cmaj7   Dm7   E♭m7   Em7   G7/D G7/B G7   C6(9)

3rd fret   5th fret   6th fret   7th fret

LESSON FIVE: *The ALTERED DOMINANT 7 chords with the root or assumed root on the ⑤ string.*

ALTERED DOMINANT 7 chords can have any combination of ♯5, ♭5, ♯9, and (or) ♭9). They can often be used as a substitute for the DOMINANT 7, especially as embellishments or in "turnarounds". They are often interchangeable. For example: if a tune calls for a C7 ♭9, in place of the ♭9, you could also possibly play: C7♯9, C7$^{(♭9)}_{(♯5)}$, C7$^{(♭9)}_{(♭5)}$, C7$^{(♯9)}_{(♭5)}$, or C7$^{(♯9)}_{(♯5)}$. However, only careful experimentation will tell you what will work and what will not work in a particular situation. Many times, strong melody notes are the altered degrees. An altered degree that works in one form may not work in another. Be prepared to resolve or move quickly to another altered degree if the one that you are playing is too dissonant.

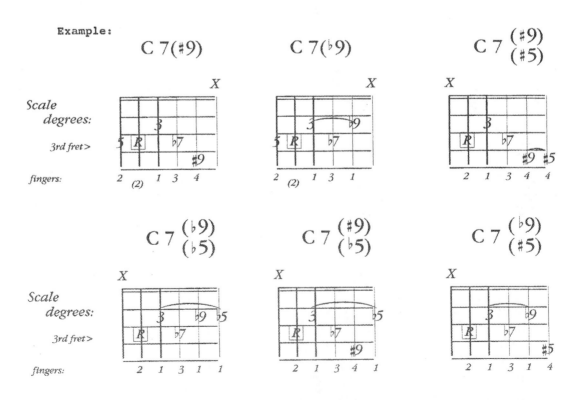

- 84 -

EXERCISE:

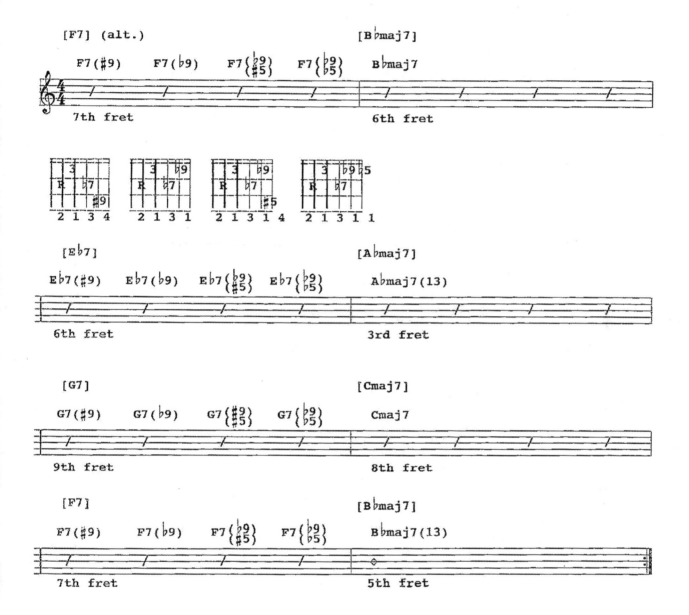

LESSON SIX: *The ALTERED DOMINANT 7 chords with the assumed root on the ⑥ string.*

You can play shortened versions of almost any chord form in this method on the first four strings. Like the three note forms, sometimes they are more practical than full forms. Such is the case with the following three.

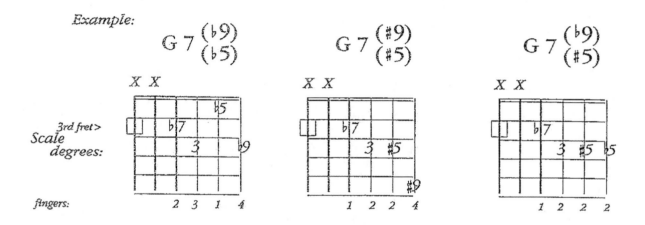

It is usually impractical to use ♭5 and ♯5 or ♭9 and ♯9 simultaneously. These chords are usually written with a keyboardist in mind. When a chord symbol calls for any of these combinations of altered degrees, substitute with one or more of the previously mentioned altered forms.

EXERCISE: An example application of ALTERED DOMINANT chords.

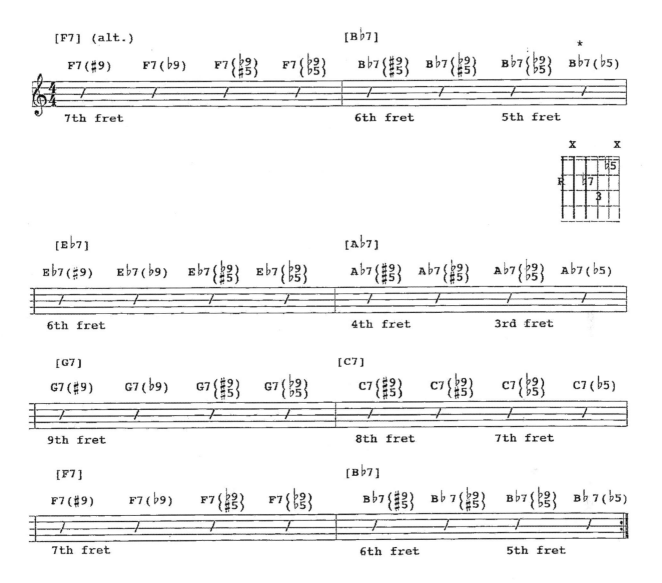

* This altered form is from page 59.

SUMMARY AND CONCLUSION

CHORD INDEX and SUBSTITUTION CHART

CHORD	PAGE	SUGGESTED SUBSTITUTION CHORDS	PAGE

MAJOR TRIADS
 	
Example:
C, D, E, etc.
	22,30
	94
		* MAJOR 6
		
		    Example: C6, D6, E6 etc.
		
		* FIRST INVERSION MAJOR TRIADS
		    (3rd in the bass)
		
		    Example: C/E, D/F♯, E/G♯ etc.
		
		MAJOR 7
		
		    Example: Cmaj7, Dmaj7, Emaj7 etc.
		
		MAJOR 6(9)
		
		    Example: C6(9), D6(9), E6(9) etc.
			56, 58
			64, 95
			
			68, 94
			
			26, 33
			39, 75
			81, 96
			
			57, 97

MAJOR 6 Example: C6, D6, E6 etc.	56, 58 64, 95	MAJOR TRIADS Example: C, D, E etc. and the same substituions as major triads	22, 30 94

SUSPENDED 4
 	
The 4th scale degree can usually be added to an open position major chord.
 	
Example:
C(sus4), D(susG), E sus
	15, 16
	95
		DOMINANT 7sus4
		
		    Example: C7sus4, D7susG, E7sus
		
		DOMINANT 7sus4(9)
		
		    Example: C7sus4(9), D7sus(9) etc.
			56, 106
			
			108

* = first choices

CHORD	PAGE	SUGGESTED SUBSTITUTION CHORDS	PAGE

AUGMENTED TRIAD
 	
Example:
C+, Daug, E ♯5
E+5
	56,
	97
		Any note in this chord can be a root. Therefore, it repeats itself every four frets.
		
		AUGMENTED 7
		
		    Example: C7(♯5), D7+5, E 7(? 13)
		
		AUGMENTED (9)
		
		    Example: C+5(9), D♯5(9), Eaug(9)
			59, 64
			106, 107
			
			109

MAJOR 7
 	
Example:
 Cmaj7, Dmaj7 etc
	26, 33
	39, 75
	81, 96
		MAJOR TRIADS
		
		    Example: C, D, E etc.
		
		MAJOR 6
		
		    Example: C6, D6, E6 etc.
		
		* MAJOR 6(9)
		
		    Example: C6(9), D6(9) etc.
		
		* MAJOR 7 $\binom{9}{13}$
		
		    Example: Cmaj(13), Dmaj(13) etc.
			22, 30
			94
			
			56, 58
			64, 95
			
			57, 97
			
			58, 96

MAJOR 7 (♯11) Example: Cmaj7(♯11) Dmaj7(+11) Emaj7(♭5) etc.	97		
MAJOR 7 altered 9 Example: Cmaj(♭9) Dmaj7(♭9) Emaj(♯9) etc.	109	MAJOR 7 Example: Cmaj7, Dmaj7, Emaj7 etc.	26, 33 39, 75 81, 96
MAJOR 9 Example: Cmaj7(9), Dmaj9 Emaj9 etc.	106	* MAJOR 7 Example: Cmaj7, Dmaj7, Emaj7 etc. and the same subs as MAJOR 7.	26, 33 39, 75 81, 96

CHORD	PAGE	SUGGESTED SUBSTITUTION CHORDS	PAGE

MINOR TRIADS
 	
Example:
Cm, D-, Em
	23, 31
	66, 98
		* MINOR 6
		
		    Example: Cm6, Dm6, E-6 etc.
		
		FIRST INVERSION MINOR TRIADS
		   (3rd in the bass)
		
		    Example: Cm/E?, Dm/F, Em/G etc.
		
		* MINOR SEQUENCES
		
		    Example: Cm, Cm(maj7), Cm7, Cm6,
		    Dm, Dm(♯5), Dm6, Dm(♯5),
		    E-, E-(maj7), E-7, E-6 etc.
			56, 59, 65
			66, 99
			
			12, 98
			
			65, 66

MINOR 6 Example: C-6, Dm6, Em6	56, 59 65, 66 99	MINOR TRIADS Example: Cm, Dm, E- etc. and the same subs as the MINOR TRIADS.	23, 31 66, 98
MINOR MAJOR 7 Example: Cm (maj7), Dm(♯7) etc.	65, 103	This chord is usually used in MINOR CHORD SEQUENCES.	

MINOR 7
 	
Example:
Cm7, D-7, Em7
	24,32,
	38,53,
	56,65,
	69,75,
	78,81,
	100,
	101
		MINOR TRIADS
		
		    Example: Cm, Dm, E- etc.
		
		and the same subs as the MINOR
		TRIADS.
		
		* MINOR 7(9)
		
		    Example: Cm7(9), Dm(9), E-9
		
		* MINOR 7$^{(9)}_{(13)}$
		
		    Example: Cm7(13), D-7(13), E-13
		
		* MINOR 7(11)
		
		    Example: Cm7(11), D-7(11) etc.
			23, 31
			66, 98
			
			54, 55, 101
			
			52, 53,
			55, 101
			
			59,102,103

CHORD	PAGE	SUGGESTED SUBSTITUTION CHORDS	PAGE
MINOR 7 (11) Example: Cm7(11), D-7(11)	59, 102.	MINOR 7 EXAMPLE: Cm7, D-7, Em7 etc. and the same subs as MINOR 7	24, 32, 56, 65, 38, 53, 69, 75, 78, 81
MINOR 7 (9) and (or) MINOR 7(13) Example: Cm7(9), Dm9 E-9 Cm7(13), Dm13 E-9(13)	54, 55, 52, 53, 55	The same as the above. (13) chords usually, but not always have a 9th degree. The 13 and 6 degree are the same note. The chord is named (13) if a ♭7 is present. It is (6) if the ♭7 is not present.	
MINOR 6(9) Example: Cm6(9), Dm6/9 E-6(9)	56, 99	MINOR TRIADS and the same subs The "ultra rich" MINOR 6(9) is best suited for endings.	23, 31 56, 59, 65, 66, 94, 95, 98, 99, 100
MINOR 7(♭5) (half diminished) Example: Cm7(♭5), Dm7-5 E⌀7 etc.	27, 35 56		
DOMINANT 7 Example: C7, D7, E7 etc.	24,35 32,39, 53,56, 68,71, 104, 105	MAJOR TRIADS Example: C, D, E etc. and the same substitutions as the MAJOR TRIADS. * DOMINANT 7(9) Example: C7(9), D(9), E9 etc. * DOMINANT 7$^{(9)}_{(13)}$ Example: C7(13), D(13), E13	22, 30 94 52, 53 107, 108 54, 55 107, 108

CHORD	PAGE	SUGGESTED SUBSTITUTION CHORDS	PAGE
DOMINANT 7 (continued)		* ALTERED DOMINANT any combination of #5(♭13), ♭5(#11), ♭9, #9 Example: C7(♭5), C7(#5), D7$\binom{\#5}{♭9}$, D7$\binom{♭5}{♭9}$, E7$\binom{\#5}{\#9}$, E7 alt.	56, 59, 64, 84, 85, 106,107, 108,109, 110,111 112,113
DOMINANT 7(9) and (or) DOMINANT 7(13) Example: C9, C7(13) C13, D7(9) D9, D13, D7(13)	52,53 54,55, 107, 108	DOMINANT 7 Example: C7, D7, E7 etc. and the same subs as DOMINANT 7	24, 25, 32, 39, 53, 56, 68, 71 104,105
DOMINANT 7(sus4) Example: C7sus4, D7(sus) E7(susA) etc.	56, 106	* DOMINANT 9(sus4) Example: C9(sus4), D9(sus), etc.	108
ALTERED DOMINANT With an altered (9) Example: C7(♭9), C7(-9) C7(#9), C7(+9) C13(♭9), C13(#9) etc.	28,36 52,84, 109, 110	Altered (9) degrees are usually interchangeable. * DOMINANT 7 Example: C7, D7, E7 etc. and most of the substitutions for DOMINANT 7.	24, 25, 32, 39, 53, 56, 68, 71, 104, 105
ALTERED DOMINANT With an altered (5)	56,59, 64,106 107	* AUGMENTED TRIADS Example: C+, D#5, Eaug etc. DOMINANT 9 with #5 or ♭5 Example: C9(#5), D9(-5), E9(+5)	56, 97, 98 108, 109

CHORD	PAGE	SUGGESTED SUBSTITUTION CHORDS	PAGE
Example: C7(♯5), C7+5 C7+, C7aug C7♭13, C9(♯5) C9+5 C7(♭5), C7(-5) C7(♯11), C9(♭5) C9(-5) etc.		Altered (5) and altered (9) degrees are often interchangeable. However, simultaneous ♯5(♭13) and ♭5(♯11) or ♭9 and ♯9 are not usually practical to play on guitar.	52

ALTERED DOMINANT
 	
With an altered (5) and an altered (9).
	52,84
	86
		* AUGMENTED TRIADS
		
		    Example: C+, D♯5, Eaug etc.
		
		    and the same as the above.
			56, 97,
			98

Example: C7{♯5}{♯9}, C7{±5}{±9},	106 107		
Caug7(+9),	108		
C7+(♯9), C+7(♯9)	109		
C7(♯5)(♭9), C7(♭5)(♭9)	110		
	111		
C7(♯11),C7(♭5)(♭9)(♯9)	112		
C7 alt.	113		

CHORD GLOSSARY

In the final pages of this method, you will find a few new chord forms and a review of the forms we have studied previously. To avoid redundancy, we will use only [G] for example. By applying the principle of movable forms, you should be able to transpose the [G] forms to almost any other chord. As I mentioned in the early pages of our studies, ALMOST EVERYTHING ABOUT GUITAR CHORDS, is not necessarily a complete study. Students should seek additional sources of information from publications, teachers, other guitarist and most of all, experience. GOOD LUCK and CONTINUE TO LEARN.

CHORD GLOSSARY Example: G

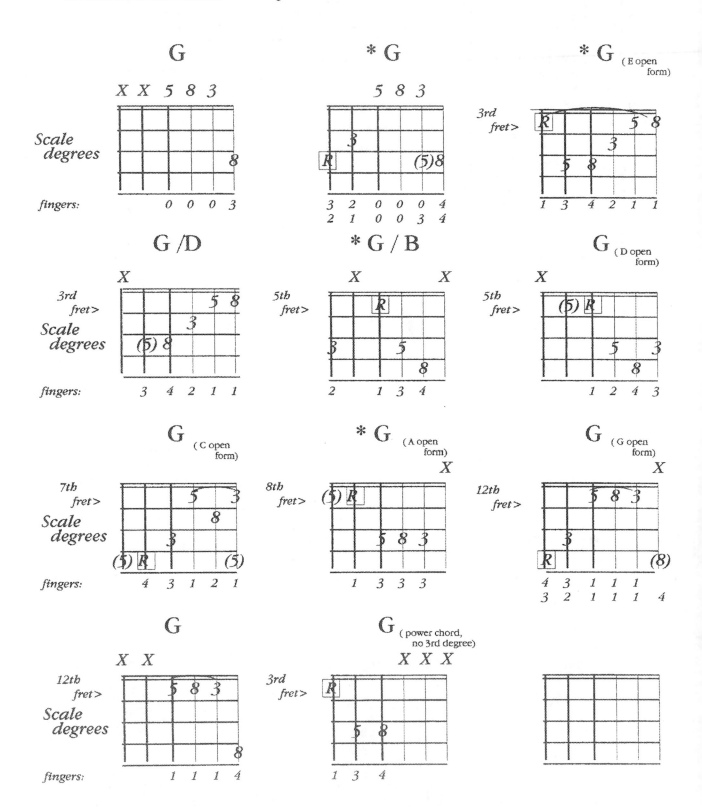

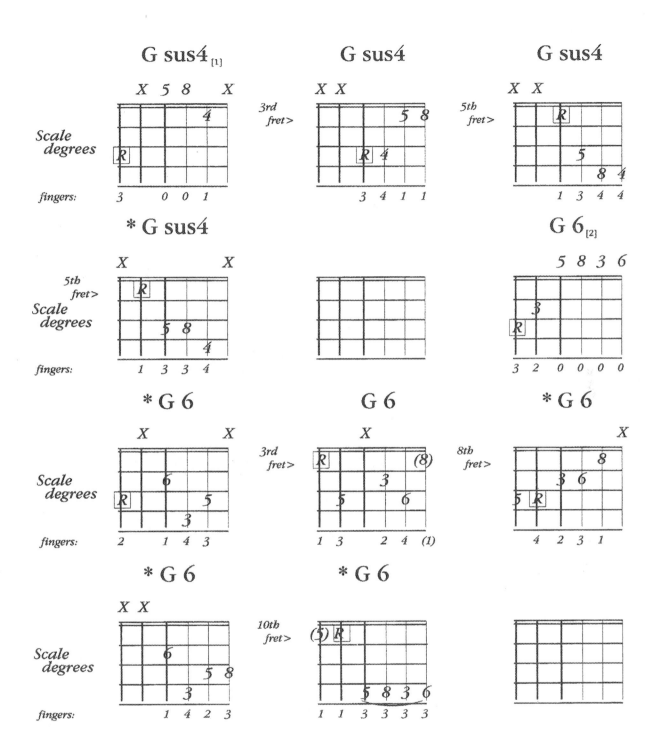

[1] SUSPENDED 4 chords do not have a 3rd degree. However, the 4th often resolves to the 3rd degree.

[2] (6) chords and MINOR 7 FIRST INVERSION have the same notes, i.e. G6 and Em7/G.

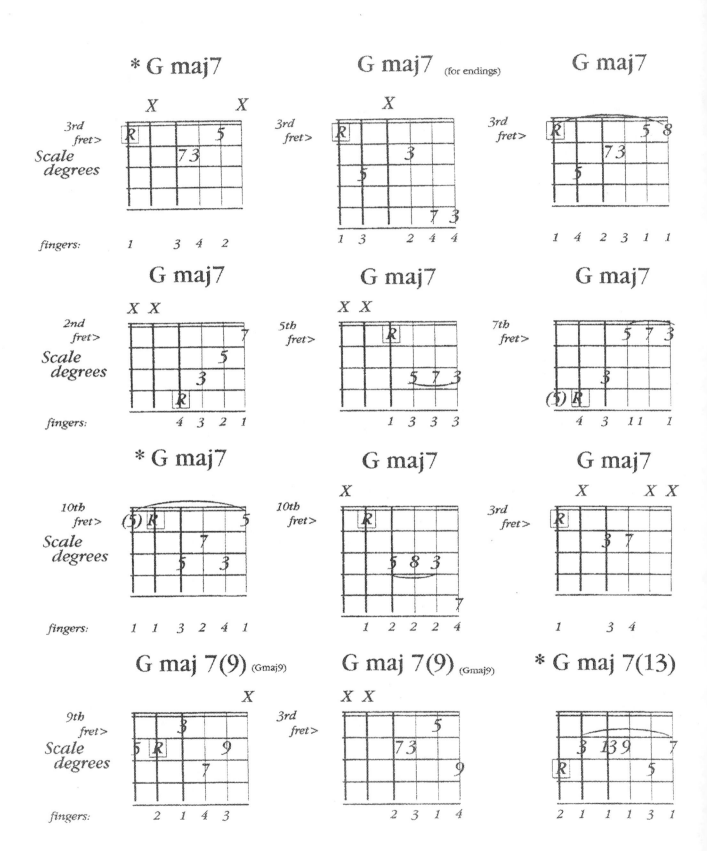

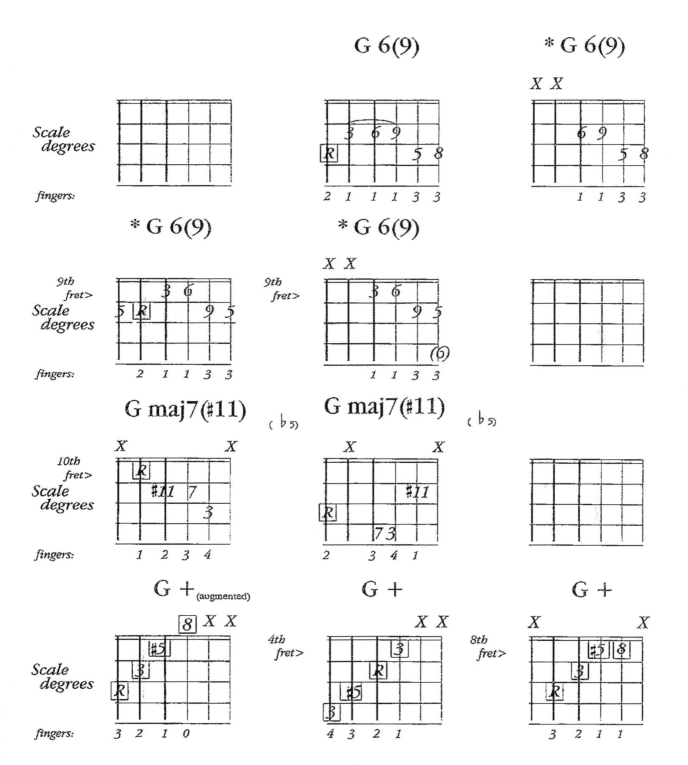

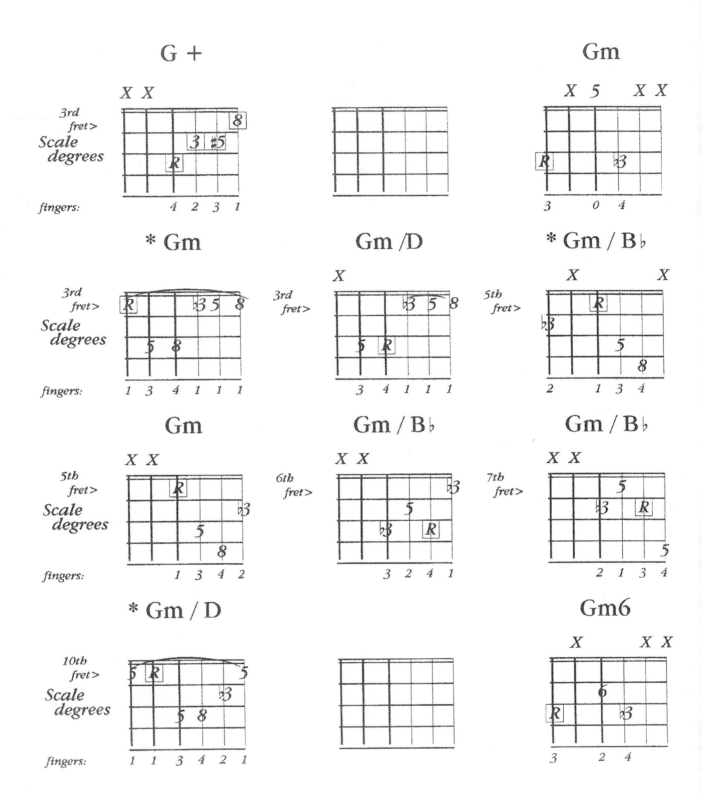

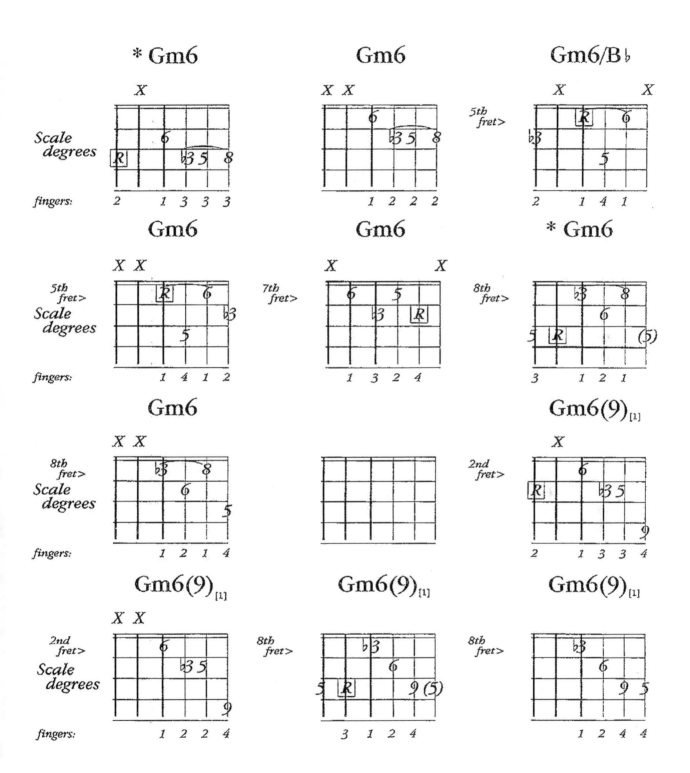

[1] The "ultra rich" MINOR 6(9) chord is best suited for endings.

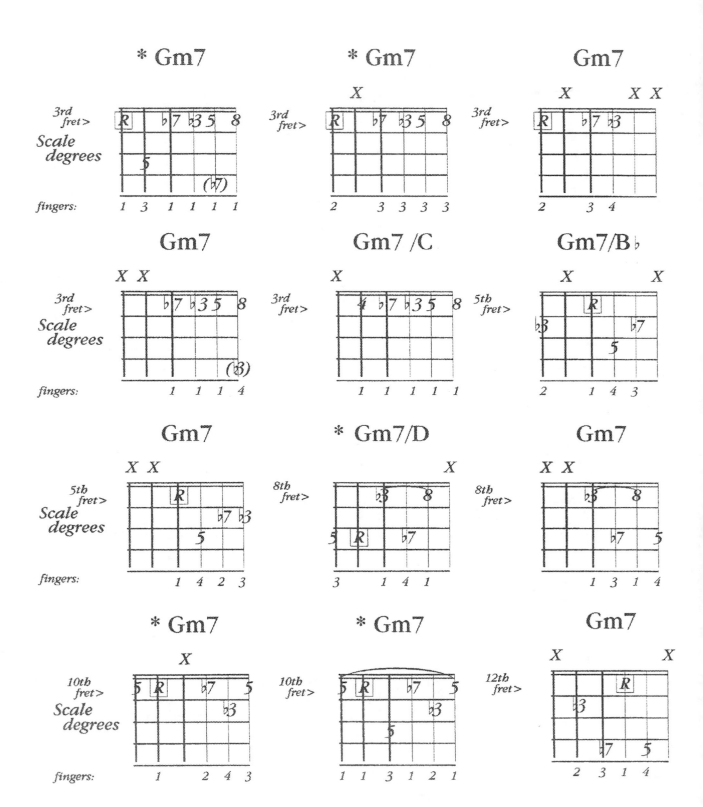

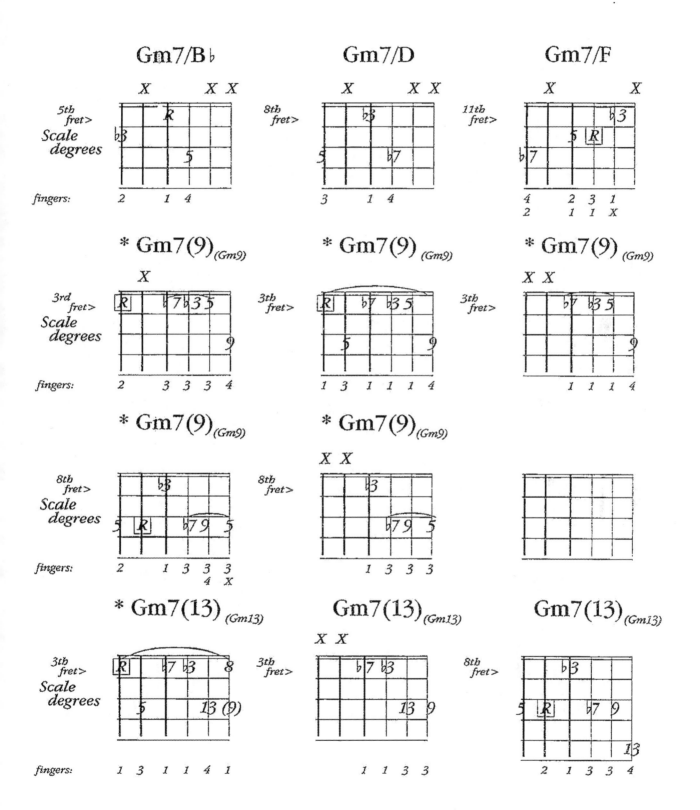

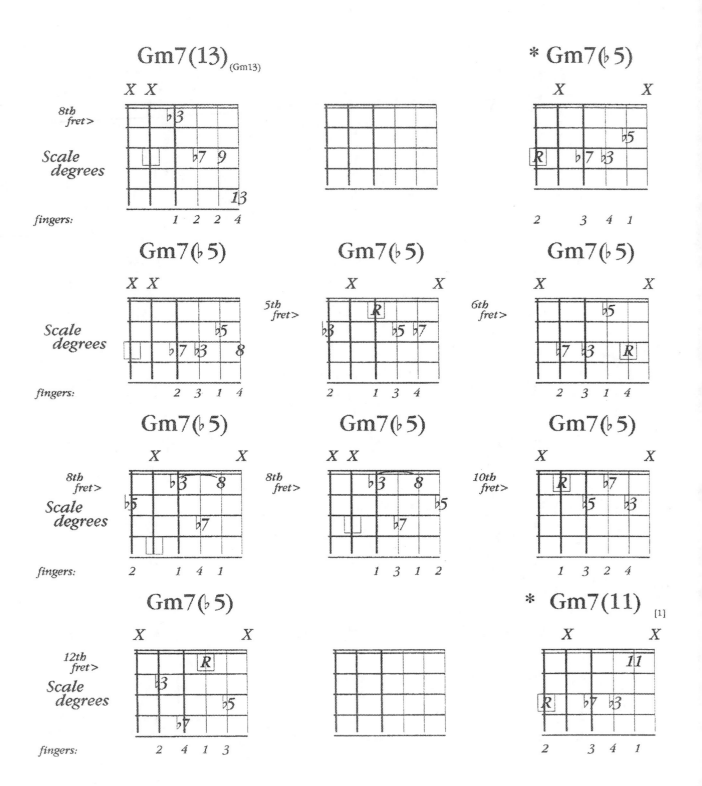

[1] The (11) and (sus4) are the same degree. The chord is
    an (11) if the 3rd is present. It is a (sus4) if the 3rd
    degree is not present.

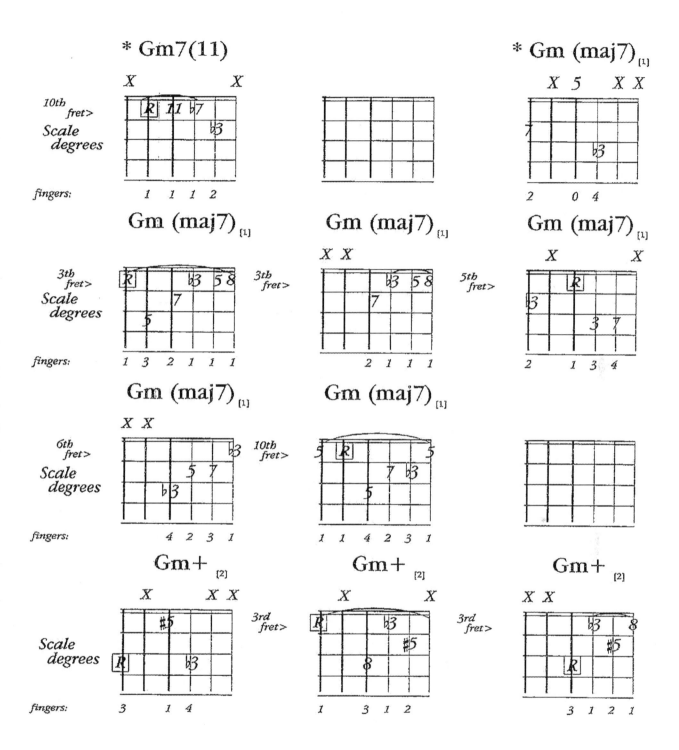

[1] The MINOR MAJOR chord is usually used in MINOR CHORD SEQUENCES. See pages 65, and 66.

[2] The AUGMENTED or #5 (+5) MINOR TRIAD is usually used in MINOR CHORD SEQUENCES. See pages 66, and 67.

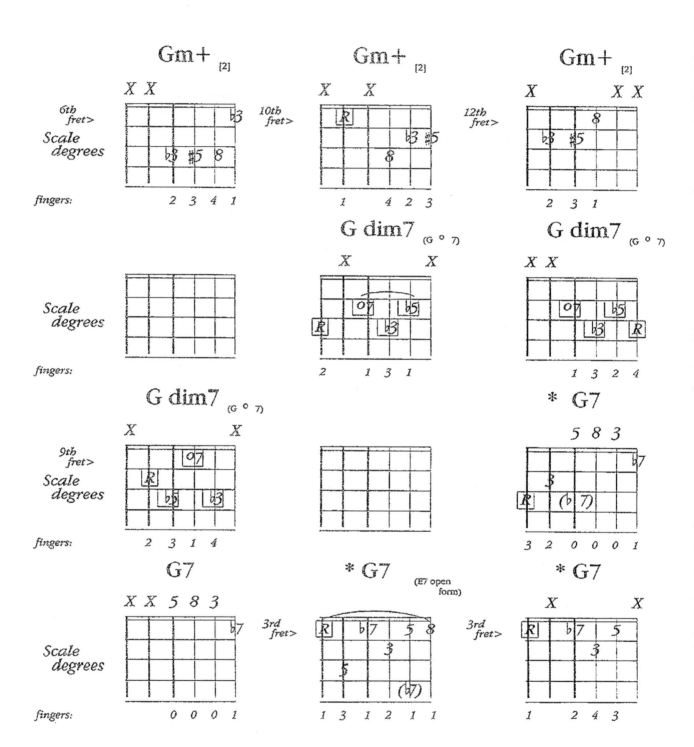

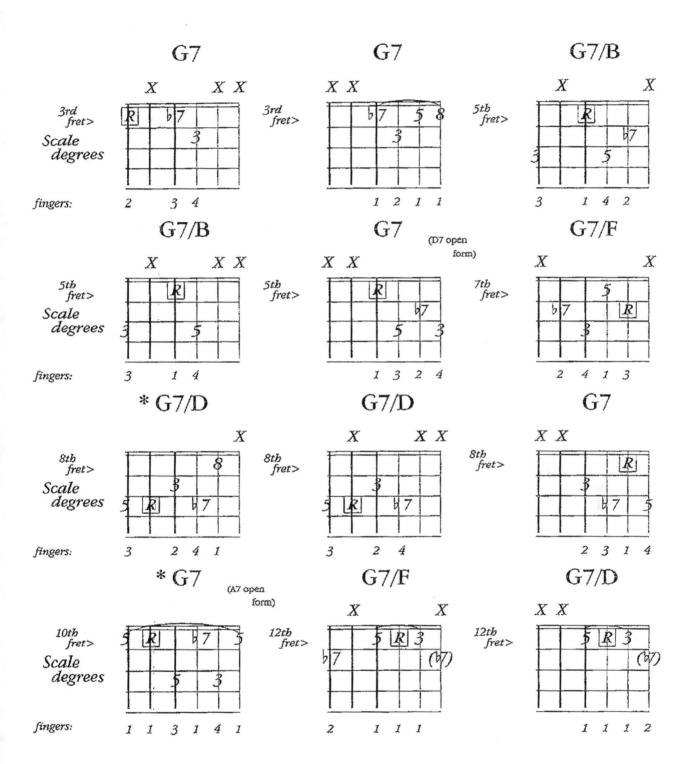

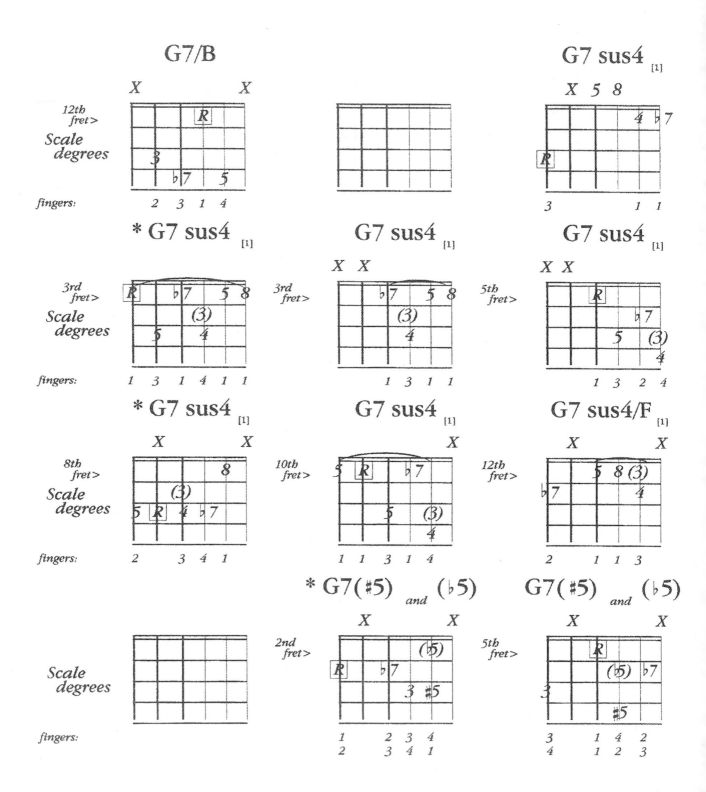

[1] The restless sounding (sus4) degree will often resolve
to the major 3.

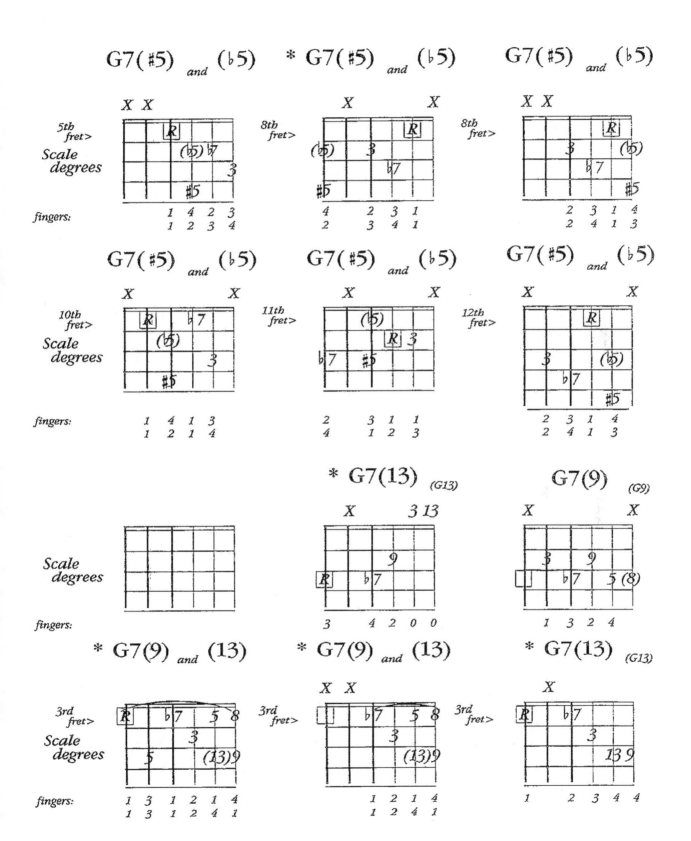

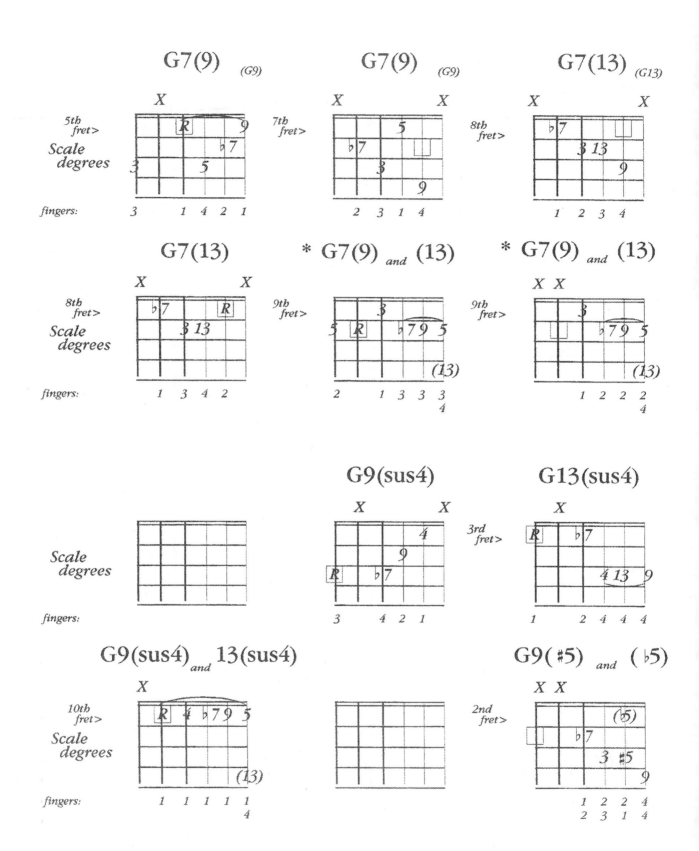

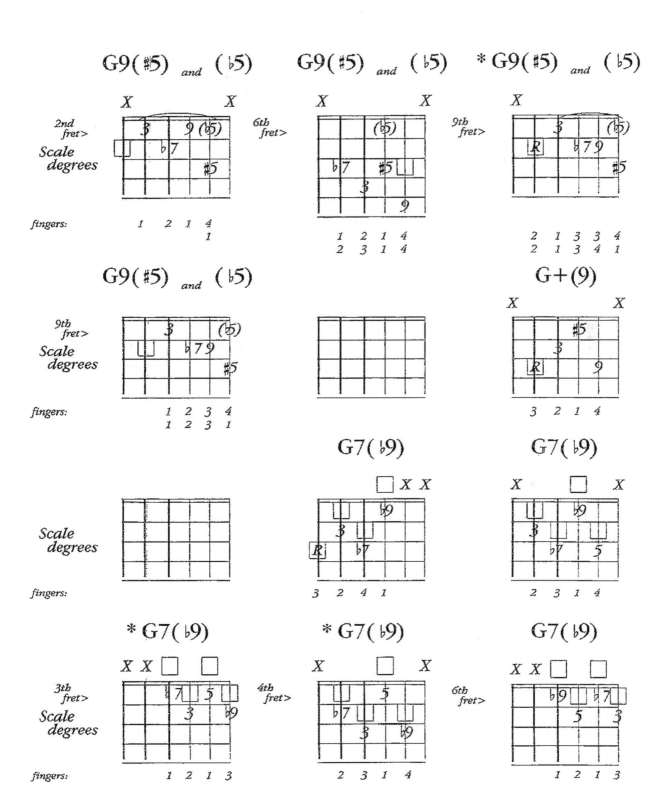

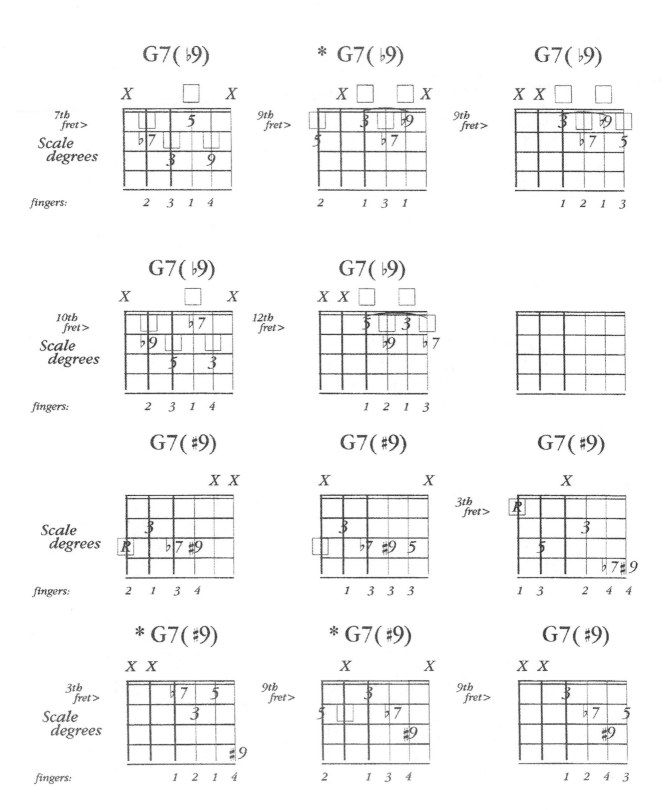

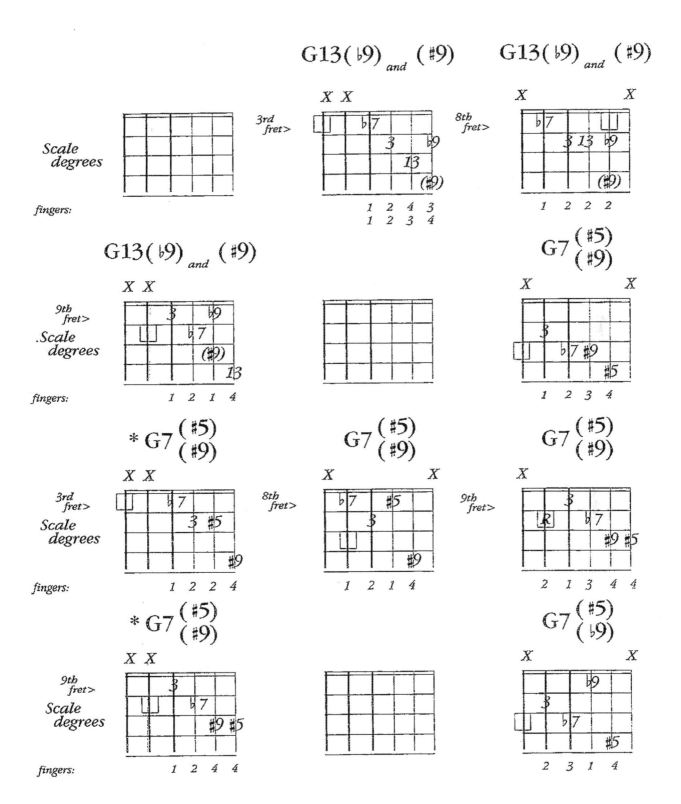

- 111 -

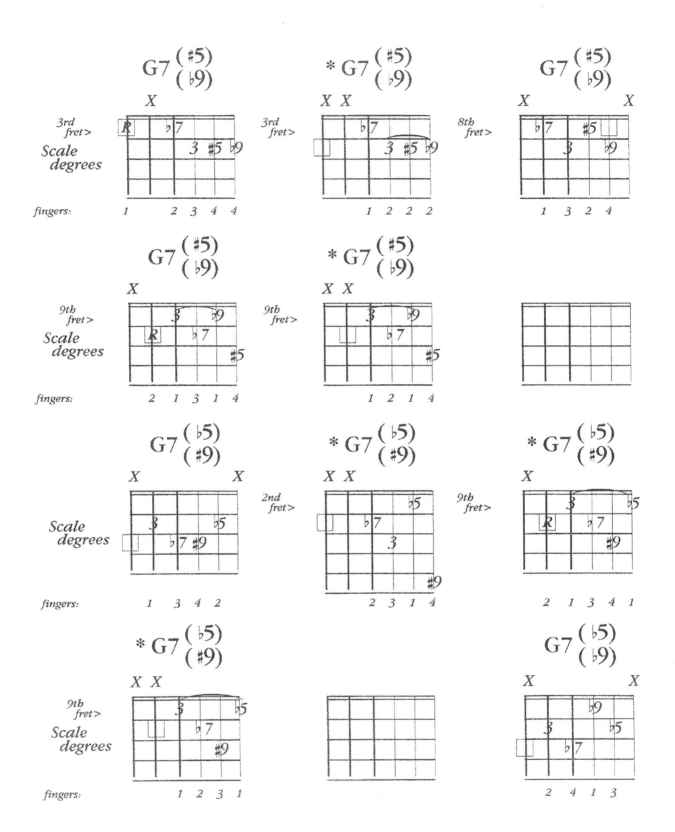

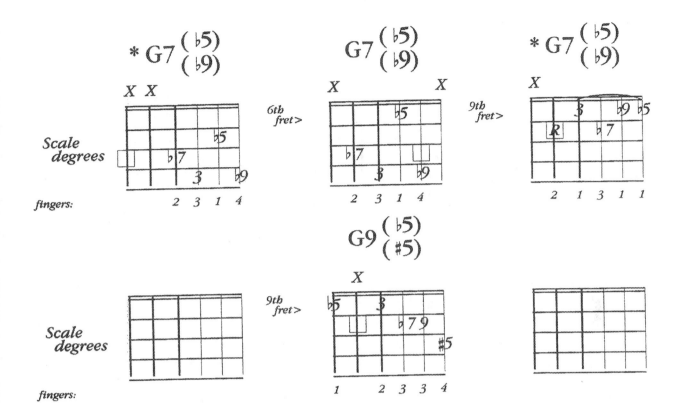

$*$ G7 $\binom{\flat 5}{\flat 9}$

Scale
degrees

fingers:

X X
             $\flat 5$
    $\flat 7$
       3    $\flat 9$
    2 3 1 4

6th
fret >

G7 $\binom{\flat 5}{\flat 9}$

X   X
        $\flat 5$
 $\flat 7$
    3   $\flat 9$
2 3 1 4

9th
fret >

$*$ G7 $\binom{\flat 5}{\flat 9}$

X
     3    $\flat 9$ $\flat 5$
 R $\flat 7$
    2 1 3 1 1

G9 $\binom{\flat 5}{\sharp 5}$

Scale
degrees

fingers:

9th
fret >

$\flat 5$ 3
      $\flat 7$ 9
        $\sharp 5$
1   2 3 3 4

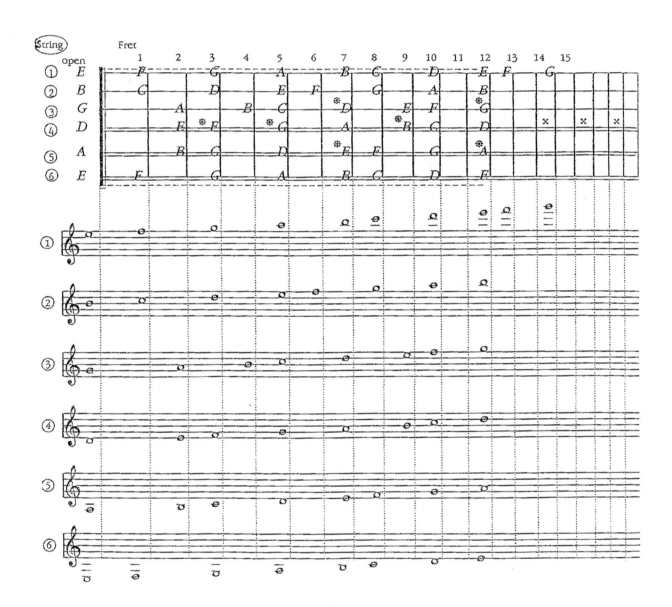

Printed in the United States
By Bookmasters